PAM GEMS

Plays Two

PAM GEMS

Plays Two

BETTY'S WONDERFUL CHRISTMAS

THE SOCIALISTS

GUINEVERE

ETHEL

Q
QUOTA BOOKS LTD
LONDON

Published in 2021 by Quota Books Ltd.
197 Hammersmith Grove, London W6 0NP

website: www.quotabooks.com – email: info@quotabooks.com
Twitter: @Quotabooks

Copyright © Pam Gems

Pam Gems is identified as the Author of the Work in accordance with Section 7 of the Copyright, Designs and Patents Act 1988. The author has asserted her moral rights.

All rights whatsoever in these plays are strictly reserved and application for performance etc. should be made before commencement of rehearsals to Rose Cobbe, United Agents, 12-26 Lexington Street, London W1F 0LE, UK. info@unitedagents.co.uk Tel: +44 (0) 20 3214 0800.

No performance may be given unless a licence has been obtained.

This book is sold subject to the condition that it shall not, by way of trade or otherwise, be lent, resold, hired out or otherwise circulated without the publisher's prior consent in any form of binding or cover other than that in which it is published and without a similar condition, including this condition, being imposed on the subsequent publisher.

A CIP record for this book is available from the British Library.

ISBN 978-1-9162460-8-9

Typeset in the UK by M Rules
Printed and bound by Biddles
Picture of Pam Gems courtesy of Jonathan Gems
Cover design: TRISTAN

Available from Amazon, Ingram Spark, Quota Books
and all politically correct bookstores.

Pam Gems was born Pamela Price in 1925, in Mudeford, near Christchurch, in what was then Dorset, on the south coast of England. Her father, a Welsh ex-coalminer, died when she was six, leaving her mother to bring up Pam and her two brothers alone.

For most of her childhood, Pam's family lived in poverty, relying on the Salvation Army and charity from the local parish church. At eleven, she won a scholarship to grammar school, where she excelled but left at fifteen to go to work.

World War Two broke out and, in 1943, when she turned eighteen, she joined the Women's Royal Naval Service, working with British and Canadian bomber squadrons. After the war, she studied psychology at Manchester University, where she met her future husband, Keith Gems.

Always stage-struck, Pam wrote her first play when she was eight, and was an enthusiastic participant in school plays. At university, she wrote for the dramatic society, along with her friend, the playwright, Robert Bolt. After university, she worked in audience research at the BBC, which she hated – but enjoyed being part of a London bohemian scene that included Sean Kenny, the theatre designer, and Ted Hughes, the poet.

After marrying and having her first two children, she moved to Wandsworth in South London, and wrote radio plays. This began a prolific writing career that produced over seventy-eight plays and adaptations. Pam Gems is Britain's greatest female playwright, with only Agatha Christie having had more West End productions.

ALSO BY THE SAME AUTHOR

Go West Young Woman
Dusa, Fish, Stas and Vi
Queen Christina
Piaf
Aunt Mary
Camille
Loving Women
Pasionaria
Deborah's Daughter
Marlene
Stanley
The Snow Palace
King Ludwig of Bavaria
Mrs. Pat
Natalya
At the Window
The Incorruptible
Franz Into April

Nelson
Garibaldi, si!
The Little Mermaid
After Birthday
Up In Sweden
Next Please
Franz Into April
My Warren
The Treat
The Amiable Courtship of Miz Venus and Wild Bill
The Synonym
The Whippet
The Russian Princess
The Burning Man
A Builder by Trade
The Nourishing Lie
Mr Watts

In Donegal
Cluster
Down West
The Country House Sale
In The Hothouse
Ladybird, Ladybird
Ebba
Guin for Guinevere
Marine
Who Is Sylvia?
The Project
You Should Be Pleased He Likes Me
What Luck
Dispatches
An Ordinary Woman
Cedric and Louise

ADAPTATIONS

The Blue Angel
Sarah B Divine!
My Name is Rosa Luxemburg
Rivers and Forests
Cheri

Uncle Vanya
A Doll's House
The Seagull
Ghosts
Yerma
The Lady from the Sea

The Cherry Orchard
Dance of Death
The Father
Hedda Gabbler
Three Sisters

NOVELS

Mrs Frampton
Bon Voyage, Mrs Frampton

CONTENTS

BETTY'S WONDERFUL CHRISTMAS   1

THE SOCIALISTS   125

GUINEVERE   203

ETHEL   291

Betty's Wonderful Christmas

BETTY'S WONDERFUL CHRISTMAS

A Christmas Play for Adults and Children

For David Aukin and Nancy Meckler

FOREWORD

BETTY'S WONDERFUL CHRISTMAS was my first stage play. The setting is a small country town between the two World Wars, when living was still harsh for many people; the Salvation Army providing the only loving support for many in real distress.

But children ran free, in safety. They knew the seasons, from broad beans to mistletoe, the names of trees, wild flowers, what was edible and what wasn't. They knew every bird that flew, every fish in the sea, and in the river. They lived off the land and sea.

A shop-bought cake was a blot on the character – although tinned pineapple was conceded as exotic birthday fare. Relationships were face-to-face – feuds and all – and no-one had a car or a telephone. Everyone walked, or rode a bike.

And everyone went to the theatre once a year – to the pantomime – which was utterly and stupendously wonderful. There was so much light and colour! Everything shone and sparkled. The Dame always had a mystifyingly deep voice and was funny. There were tricks and jokes and pies pushed, rather worryingly, into people's faces. The story always came out right, and the only boring moments were when everything stopped for a song.

At our little church school, we did plays too. I remember standing in the school playground, watching tinsel-edged tarlatan wings being fixed to the fairies' backs, and the strong smell of the Leichner sticks, with a strange feeling of familiarity – of coming home.

So, writing a play for children seemed the way to begin – with a big cast, lots of adventures, music, jokes, and scene changes.

FOREWORD

Ignorance is bliss.

But I was lucky. The young David Aukin, as his first producing venture, was mounting a repertory of plays at the Cockpit Theatre over Christmas, and needed a show for the matinées.

The fair, fragile Yvonne Antrobus played Betty and looked 14 (She was married and a mother.) We had funky music from a trio who also played roles in the show, and we played in the round – so close to the audience that the Dragon's four-year-old son ran onstage in protest when his father's tail was stamped on.

It was the best of entrées – a group of lively, irreverent and inventive actors, trained and talented, solving the problems of a beginner's text. The actress playing the Queen said one morning: "I hope you've got something else on the stocks. You're going to miss all this when we stop. Get your pen out."

It was good advice, and I took it.

To Ann Mitchell, my thanks.

Pam Gems

REVIEWS

"Betty's Wonderful Christmas, by Pam Gems, is offered to "older children and adults." But I am not sure that it is for children at all. Not because of its extreme harshness, and not even because of its range of adult references, but because it seems the kind of fairy tale written out of adult experience by someone who preserves the mechanics and furniture of the pre-adolescent imagination. Less a piece for children than the work of a prodigious child.

In form, it passes from a slice of nightmarish life to a romantic dream. Though, in fact, the dream is hardly any more fantastic than the reality, which amounts to a nineteenth century world of puffed-up clergymen, savage domestic poverty, and street prowlers, through which the fatherless heroine wanders in a pitiful paper dress. It is like Hans Christian Anderson rewritten by George Gissing.

Fleeing from a humiliating party, Betty falls into a prowler's clutches, and the piece enters its dream zone – conveyed quite magically in Roland Rees's production by a solo flute, and the slow descent from above of a garlanded pavilion. Figures from the first part return in various transfigurations, pointing her way on a fabulous journey towards an eligible prince.

But his court turns out to be a grand-scale replay of the Christmas Party. And, he himself, a shuffling replica of a potato man from the winter streets.

The story, in short, is built on the childhood 'and then' principle. But there is nothing in the least bit childish in its use of dream logic, and its Freudian resolution.

As a writer, Miss Gems mixes in scenes of horse-trading, upper-class satire, colour supplement gags, words taboo to juveniles, and anything else that appeals to her.

REVIEWS

It might be chaotic to read, but most of it works brilliantly in the production, which has the courage to cantilever a fantasy out of thin air, and create its own consistent world where trees grow both oranges and apples, and a wild polka in 1920's dresses with long cigarette-holders clamped in the teeth, reaches its climax with a gunshot blackout and the Gothic invasion.

The production is splendidly designed by Douglas Heap. There are excellent quick-change performances from Pip Donaghy and Ann Mitchell, but the mainstay of the show is Yvonne Antrobus's Betty."

Irving Wardle. *The Times*. 6/1/1972

"I've got to know the dark side of the moon" is a song at the beginning of the play, and this is the theme for the play. BETTY'S WONDERFUL CHRISTMAS takes off from a sub-Dickensian world of paupers and charity loaves into a mesmeric phantasmagoria of Goths, holiday camps, magic forests, and whole-food commercials.

The story, as such, is incidental. The play's impact is in the atmospherically strong incidents, expertly directed by Roland Rees, with a highly talented company. My worry was that gags about the League of Nations and wheat-germ would only make the most erudite of kids fall about, and therefore I was going to give it qualified approval. But! My five-year-old son informs me that he liked it much better than the Paper Bag Players, so I must be wrong. Visually, the play is a real treat, and there's action galore. But it's not instant escapism since, throughout, the darker reality of events crashes in. Here's one puzzled parent thinking about what his son is thinking about – and that's possibly the best recommendation for the play there is."

Time Out. 17/1/1972

BETTY'S WONDERFUL CHRISTMAS was first presented at the Cockpit Theatre, Gateforth Street, London NW8, December 19 1971–January 21 1972. Produced by David Aukin.

<u>CAST</u>

(in alphabetical order)

Betty	YVONNE ANTROBUS
Betty's brother/ Page/ Boy Wally	ROBIN BALDWIN
Policeman/ Rich father Curate/ Prince Peter	STEPHEN BRADLEY
Potato man/ Lonicera/ Prince Arthur	PIP DONAGHY
Gladys Warchurch/ Patricia Seaward-Isles/ Sexy sunbather/ Singer	MARGURITE HARDIMAN
Verger/Sir Horse Chestnut/ Gardener/ Dragon	CHARLES HYATT
Bellamy/ Phyllis/ Lady Selina/ Queen's daughter	FRANCES LEE
Mother/ Mrs Spring-in-Winter/ Queen	ANN MITCHELL
Alf Silver/ Goth	RICHARD PENDRY
Salvation Army Major/ Mrs Honeywell/ Lady Fay	HONOR SHEPHERD
Musicians	HUGH FRASER
	HUGH SHEPHERD
	TIM THOMAS
Lyrics	JONATHAN GEMS
Director	ROLAND REES
Designer	DOUGLAS HEAP

BETTY'S WONDERFUL CHRISTMAS

CHARACTERS

BETTY, a poor girl
MAJOR FOSTER, of the Salvation Army
SALVATION ARMY LADY
THE MOTHER
BETTY'S BROTHER #1
BETTY'S BROTHER #2
POTATO MAN
ERRAND BOY
POLICEMAN
VERGER
MAID
GIRL#1
GIRL#2
ROUGH BOY
BOY ANDERSON
BOY MURPHY
MRS JONES
SMALL BOY
WALLY
MRS HONEYWELL
FARMER'S WIFE
MRS BEECH
MRS FINCH
PATRICIA SEAWARD-ISLES
GIRL GLADYS WARCHURCH
GIRL PHYLLIS
VICAR
FOOTMAN #1

FOOTMAN #2
COURTIER #1
COURTIER #2
CHANCELLOR
LADY FAY
MESSENGER
OLD COURTIER
PSEUDO PRINCE
DWARF #1
DWARF #2
EVGENIA
ANNUNZIATA
KING
ALF SILVER
MRS SPRING-IN-WINTER
LONICERA FRAGRANTISSIMA
SIR HORSE CHESTNUT
ACORN JOCKEY
GARDENER
LADY-IN-WAITING
PAGE
PRINCE PETER
PRINCE ARTHUR
LADY SELINA
THE QUEEN
QUEENS' DAUGHTER
MAESTRO
PEASANT #1
PEASANT #2
SOLDIER #1
SOLDIER #2
SOLDIER #3
OLD MAN

BETTY'S WONDERFUL CHRISTMAS

NURSE #1
NURSE #2
CAPTAIN
FRIAR
REDCOAT #1
REDCOAT #2
THE CAPTAIN OF THE GOTHS
A DRAGON
GOTH #1
GOTH #2
GOTH #3
GOTH #4
PRETTY MAID #1
PRETTY MAID #2
MAN IN SUIT
WELL-DRESSED LADY
PRELATE
VILLAGER #1
VILLAGER #2

The play may be performed by a cast of twenty-three – 7 women, 8 men, 4 girls, 4 boys.

BETTY'S WONDERFUL CHRISTMAS

ACT ONE

<u>ACT ONE SCENE ONE</u>

The settings can be what you will. If naturalistic, they would comprise a terrace of modest houses, with similar rows suggested behind – each with a lighted Christmas tree in the window, forming a pattern – up to a deep blue sky and the evening star.

The street is part of a small square, with a church porch down right. In the foreground, a POTATO MAN sells hot potatoes. They are real, and so is the smell. It is snowing lightly and people pass, heads down, carrying parcels.

A laughing family crosses, carrying a goose and a Christmas tree. Their clothes are Early Twenties, long skirts, soft hair low on the brow, the children in low-belted coats and large felt hats.

Out of the vestry come the VERGER and the local POLICEMAN. They set up a trestle table, panting and grumpy, and load up large loaves of bread – tin-shaped.

BETTY enters with an enormous bundle of washing. She is thirteen years old, and an unprepossessing sight in reach-me-down clothes and cast-off boots. Her thin, mousy hair is short, parted at the side with a gaunt hair slide.

An ERRAND BOY passes. He may be on a bike, his basket laden, or running, the basket on his arm. He sends her flying.

                    BETTY

                    (Sprawled over her bundle.)

            Hey! Look where you're going!

Her voice is hoarse, adenoidal and rustic. The BOY's answer is inaudible, but sounds rude.

                    BETTY

            I'll scrag you too!

The smell of potatoes is irresistible. She goes to the POTATO MAN, but he waves her away irritably. She approaches the bread table, and watches the loaves being piled up.

                    BETTY

            Shall I help you, Mr Thistlethwaite?

                    VERGER

            Out of my way, girl. Six o'clock we give out the bread
            and not before.

The POLICEMAN stands with his thumbs in his belt.

                    POLICEMAN

            Ah, they all expects to be waited on nowadays. They
            has too much done for them. When I was a boy, it was
            Work! We knew what it was all about. Up at five. Cows
            milked by six. Hard work! Work never harms you!

He crosses, waddling importantly.

                    BETTY

                    (Sotto voce.)

            What a whopper!

He turns, suspicious. She humps her bundle to a door and knocks. No reply. She thunders on the door. A window flies up and a MAID looks out.

ACT ONE

MAID

(Bawls)

Who is it?

BETTY

(Sing-song, her trade call.)

Washing, Miss!

MAID

Leave it on the step.

She slams down the window.

BETTY

(Same sing-song)

Shilling, please!

She knocks again. The window flies up.

MAID

What is it now?

BETTY

Me Mum'll give me the copper stick if I don't get the shilling!

MAID

Oh, wait a minute.

She returns to the window and throws down the shilling crossly.

BETTY

The lady gives me a penny. Tuppence at Christmas!

MAID

And thruppence for cheek, I suppose!

She bangs down the window. CHILDREN are gathering for the bread.

VERGER

Come on, come on, you lot. We haven't got all night.

BETTY

(To rough boy.)

Get out of it.

He pushes her. She makes a face but steers clear of the bully. A WELL-DRESSED MAN enters with TWO LITTLE GIRLS in fur-trimmed hats and muffs.

WELL-DRESSED MAN

Two nice hot potatoes, please!

GIRL #1

Thank you, Daddy!

GIRL #2

Scrumptious! We'd better keep our gloves on!

They squeal and giggle. BETTY mimics them soundlessly.

POTATO MAN

(Unctuously)

There you are, my dears. Mind your fingers. Thank you, sir. Thank you indeed! And a happy Christmas to you!

WELL-DRESSED MAN

And to you!

GIRLS

Happy Christmas! Happy Christmas!

They go.

BETTY

Go on, give us a littl'un.

ACT ONE

POTATO MAN

Buzz off.

BETTY

You ain't going to sell all those – they'll be wasted.

POTATO MAN

Clear off out of it before I call the bobby.

VERGER

Where's my list? Who's had my list? Put that down, boy. Oh, my dear – what a lot of riff-raff.

Enter the POLICEMAN.

POLICEMAN

You boys behave yourselves or you'll get your heads clouted. Take your loaves and go home.

VERGER

Anderson ...

ANDERSON

Yessir.

VERGER

Two loaves for Anderson.

ANDERSON

Thankee, sir.

The POLICEMAN holds ANDERSON by the ear.

POLICEMAN

You tell your father Mr Peach wants his horse back. Do you hear me, boy?

ANDERSON

(Going.)

Yessir!

VERGER

Murphy. Is it four for Murphy?

MURPHY

Thank you Mr Thwithlethwaite!

He makes off, sinking his teeth ravenously into the top loaf.

VERGER

Bellamy. Where's Bellamy?

BELLAMY, a small girl is pushed forward. She hides the loaves under her shawl, ashamed.

ROUGH BOY

Go on. Who's father's in the workhouse?

BETTY moves fast, swiftly kicking the ROUGH BOY. He yells, and twists her arm. The POLICEMAN looms, and he melts.

VERGER

Butler. Two loaves. Butler – stop kicking the table, boy. They do want to irritate you. That's all they want. Betty Butler!

BETTY stumbles through.

VERGER

Look at those hands, girl! Mother's supposed to be a washerwoman. Pity she don't start on her kids!

BETTY

(Shouts)

You leave my mother alone!

The VERGER looks up at the snow, and he and the POLICEMAN carry the table into the vestry, 'helped' by the CHILDREN.

ACT ONE

BETTY makes off with her loaves, head down. The ROUGH BOY, a loaf under each arm, dodges from the church, and trips her from behind. He makes off with one of her loaves.

BETTY

Hey, give it back! You rooking thief! Give it back!

POTATO MAN

Serves you right!

BETTY

What for? I haven't done nothing! He pinched my loaf! My Mum'll murder me!

POTATO MAN

Nah, kids.

BETTY

Yeah, kids! If it wasn't for us kids nobody else would buy your rotten old spuds. They're all last year's stuff – only fit for pigs!

POTATO MAN

You shut your yap-hole. I don't take any notice of squits like you. *(Complete change of tone to the greasy.)* Hullo, Mrs!

MRS JONES has entered with a SMALL BOY who has a chamber-pot stuck on his head. However, he is wearing his best clothes.

MRS JONES

Here's the potato man, Albie. Have a spud and shut your poor little gob. Look at him, Mr Mould. 'Tis pitiful. It's a bleeding shame for this to happen to a boy, I say.

POTATO MAN

Hullo, Mrs Jones. Whatever's the matter with your Albie? What's he done to himself?

BETTY

Anybody normal could see what he's done!

MRS JONES

(Buying a potato)

I feel so ashamed. It would be different if it was a saucepan, or a vase. A vase would be respectable! Suppose a policeman saw us! I didn't go into wedlock to be seen on the streets with a boy looking like this.

BETTY

He can't help it!

MRS JONES

(Gives potato to her son.)

Oh, hullo, Betty. Well, I wouldn't like a child of mine to see such a sight... *(Whispers to the POTATO MAN)* ... especially a little girl...

BETTY

What I'm supposed to be? Put his cap on, then it won't show so much. *(She grabs the cap that he's holding and places it on top of the chamber-pot.)* There! It hardly notices! *(Sotto voce.)* Give us a bite.

MRS JONES

That's better, Albie!

ALBIE holds out the spud to BETTY. But his mother snatches it.

MRS JONES

Don't be so filthy. *(To BETTY.)* He don't mean it, dear. He's a boy.

ACT ONE

BETTY is left with her mouth open as they scurry off. The POTATO MAN begins to pack up his stand.

BETTY

Go on. Give us a little 'un. Hey, haepenny for that 'un.

POTATO MAN

You show us the money – then you'll get him.

She proffers a halfpenny. He picks over his potatoes, finding a smallish one. Decides it is too big and picks out a smaller.

BETTY

Wah! Look at that! I need me glasses to see that!

POTATO MAN

Well, if you don't want it ...

She pops it in her mouth as he holds out his hand. It is hot and she hops about, throwing the halfpenny on the ground for him to grovel. Which he does, diligently.

BETTY

Go on, Mouldie. Look for it! Ooh ... Ah! It ain't half hot! My tongue! Bums up, Mouldie!

POTATO MAN

(Shocked.)

Don't be so rude! I'll tell your mother on you, using a word like that!

BETTY

Like what?

POTATO MAN

You knows what you said. I ain't repeating it.

BETTY

I never said nothing.

POTATO MAN

Then you're a liar.

BETTY

(To the audience.)

I never said nothing, did I?

POTATO MAN

Yes, you did. You said ...

BETTY

What did I say? What did I say? *(To the audience.)* I never said nothing, did I? What did I say?

If the children in the audience say the word, then this gives the POTATO MAN his affronted exit. If not, he goes off, spitting nastily at BETTY as he passes.

BETTY's spirits sink.

BETTY

All right for you! My Mum's going to kill me! Only one loaf.

She looks down at its brother, which now looks pecked, as she has been absently picking at it.

BETTY

And he looks as if a donkey's put his head over the hedge and had a bite. Perhaps if I put a bit of dirt on it, it'll look like the crust.

She rubs the loaf in the gutter.

BETTY

That's better. *(She takes another look, and is less sure.)* I could say I was run over and the wheels just missed me and went over the loaf!

ACT ONE

She turns to go, reinforced by her story, and is caught up in the stream of the SALVATION ARMY and followers – with LANTERNS and a SMALL BAND. She lurches out of the way and draws close.

MAJOR FOSTER

Right friends. "While Shepherds Watched."

BOY

We've had that twice, Major Foster!

MAJOR FOSTER gives him a quelling look, and lifts his hands to give the beat. BETTY dodges, as if expecting a blow.

MAJOR FOSTER

Don't be frightened, child. I'm your friend. What's your name?

BETTY

Betty Butler, sir.

MAJOR FOSTER

Dear Lord, we bid welcome to this poor child, who comes to worship Thee. Here's a penny, Betty. Worship the Lord. Where do you live?

WOMAN ONE

The mother's a widow. Lives in Pound Lane.

BOY

Waw! Do you live down Stink Alley?

WOMAN TWO

Feller went to a stick in six months. Galloping consumption – that's what he had. He was a big man, but not when he finished.

WOMAN ONE

You could see his face when you went past the workhouse. Hullo, I'd say. But he'd never answer.

WOMAN TWO

That's right. Just sit at the window, crying. Not a bit of noise. Just the tears running down his face. For his kids, you see? He missed tem. They wouldn't let him see them. Well, you can't have kids in there – all their noise.

MAJOR FOSTER

Do you remember your father, Betty?

BETTY

(Without expression)

Yes sir.

MAJOR FOSTER looks at her.

MAJOR FOSTER

While Shephard's Watched.

He lifts his hands. They sing the carol.

MAJOR FOSTER

Now friends, we move on to the mission for a short service. Would you like to come, Betty, and worship the Lord? There's a sausage supper after!

BETTY

I've got to take the bread home, sir.

BOY

That's Church of England bread, Major Foster. That's a charity loaf she got there.

WOMAN THREE

(Shocked)

C of E?

Fierce disapproval. MAJOR FOSTER waves a restraining hand. He puts his hand on BETTY's shoulder.

ACT ONE

MAJOR FOSTER

May the Lord lead you into righteousness.

BETTY

I only goes for the bread.

MAJOR FOSTER

Take it home, my dear.

They go.

BETTY

Now I'm for it.

BETTY begins to move off. There is a noise behind her. She turns.

BETTY

Who is it?

No-one. She turns, and makes off. Then she hears a step, and turns again sharply.

BETTY

(Stoutly.)

I knows who it is! Buzz off, you!

Silence. She makes off, calling over her shoulder.

BETTY

I ain't afraid of you!

But she takes to her heels. Pause. Then a MAN crosses the stage, monstrous and ominous – on the hunt. BETTY crosses to an almost paint-less door. She listens, then lifts the latch very gently. Just as she has successfully opened the door, it is wrenched from within, and she is yanked out of sight.

MOTHER

Get in!

We see nothing but the whirl of an old shawl, followed by the brandishing of a copper stick. The door slams, and we hear BETTY's hoarse screams and shouts.

Light change.

ACT ONE SCENE TWO

Betty's Home.

The room is squalid and untidy with damp walls and peeling wallpaper. There is a tiny range, a deal table, chairs with no backs, and a lot of washing. TWO SMALL BOYS, named MICK and DERRY) sit at table, waiting for their tea. BETTY sniffles in a corner.

Her MOTHER attacks the loaf with a large knife.

MOTHER

Don't think you're getting any! You've eaten one loaf, you're not getting another!

BETTY

He took it. I told you.

MOTHER

(Hissing over her, knife in hand.)

Then you're a little liar, as usual, aren't you?

BETTY

(Frightened.)

Cut it out!

The MOTHER suddenly collapses. She droops, ashamed of herself, and deep in depression. She moves away.

ACT ONE

MOTHER

(Mutters)

Get in your seat if you want something.

BETTY

I don't want nothing.

MOTHER

No, you're getting another meal, aren't you? *(To the BOYS.)* She's going to a party.

BETTY

What?

BETTY looks up. She has conveniently forgotten.

MOTHER

You're going down to the Honeywell's aren't you?

BETTY

No, I'm not. I said I wasn't going.

MOTHER

Someone else can feed you for a change. See if they can keep up with you.

BETTY

I'm not going.

MOTHER

You are – and you'd better hurry up about it.

BETTY

(A fierce howl.)

I can't go. I got nothing to wear. You can't go to a party without you got a party dress!

MOTHER

(Tight.)

You'll wear what you're told.

BETTY

That's not a party dress. Her mother made it for the carnival. It's made of paper! You can't wear a paper dress in the middle of winter.

MOTHER

You'll do as you're told.

BETTY

It's an old cast-off carnival dress.

MOTHER

And you can stop that.

BETTY

She wore it for Bo Peep!

MOTHER

(Shouting.)

And get yourself washed!

BETTY

I've told you. I'm not going. Who ever heard of going to a Christmas party in a paper dress. They'd all laugh at me! All very well for you. You're not the one's going to get laughed at.

MOTHER

(Quiet and tight.)

I've told you, and you'd better hurry up, I shan't tell you again. *(Shouts)* Get washed!

ACT ONE

BETTY

(Very brave.)

I'm not going.

Her MOTHER moves like lightning. She leaps on BETTY. Hurls her out of the room, and a bucket after her. The bucket clanks. There is a moment's silence, then BETTY hammers on the door.

BETTY

(Offstage, pleading.)

Mum! ... Mu-um!

The MOTHER eats, stiffly. The BOYS watch. She gets them some rice pudding from an old, burnt enamel bowl. They fall on it, eating until their plates shine. BETTY staggers in with a bucket of water. She pours some into a bowl and tops it up from the kettle to take the chill off. She washes in the corner. The boys whisper. BETTY turns away to wash her crotch, and reaches for her petticoat.

BETTY

(Timid.)

Did you do me a clean petticoat?

MOTHER

What do you think I am, your lackey? She thinks I've got nothing better to do!

BETTY

This one stinks.

MOTHER

I'm not surprised.

BETTY puts on the old, sagging garment. DERRY cackles – but withers at his MOTHER's glare. The MOTHER takes something from the cupboard.

MOTHER

Here.

BETTY

What?

MOTHER

What does it look like? Clean pair of socks.

BETTY

Socks.

MOTHER

Ankle socks. Well, you can't wear black woollen stockings with a party dress. These cost me seven pence farthing.

BETTY

But it's too cold! I ain't half cold out!

MOTHER

And how far away are they? Not more than half a mile. You can run, can't you? I never had ankle socks!

BETTY

All very well for you – stuck in here, in the warm.

Her MOTHER pushes her against the table.

BETTY

Ow!

BETTY puts on the socks.

BETTY

Can I lend your shoes?

The MOTHER groans but takes them off. BETTY is pleased. The shoes have a slight heel. The effect is appalling. Suddenly, she remembers the dress and her spirits sag.

ACT ONE

BETTY

(*With great gallantry.*)

All right. Where is it?

Her MOTHER fetches a paper bag. Takes out a blue paper dress, the skirt formed of three gathered flounces. There is tinsel at the waist and neck. She holds it up, and her face softens, enchanted by it. She holds it up against BETTY, then helps her carefully into it.

BETTY flinches at her first touch, but then submits when she realizes it is not to be a clout. She stands still as her MOTHER fastens the back, and smooths out the skirt. The dress is slightly too small.

BETTY

It would have to be blue!

MOTHER

It's a beautiful colour. It looks very nice.

BETTY

Just as well I can't see it myself.

She goes to the mantelpiece, finds a piece of comb, and begins to tug at her hair.

MOTHER

Oh, come here!

She combs her daughter's hair. BETTY responds to this. She begins to relax and preen. Whereupon her MOTHER jerks her cruelly. BETTY howls.

MOTHER

Oh, finish it yourself. She won't keep still. What's the matter now?

BETTY

Lost me slide.

She gropes about on the floor.

MICK

She'll never get there.

BETTY

(Vicious)

Don't you worry, four-eyes. I'm having jelly and cake. More than you're getting, so buzz off!

She fixes her slide.

MOTHER

Let's have a look at you.

They regard each other – the faded, once-pretty woman, and her plain child.

MOTHER

My God, what does she look like? Look at her petticoat hanging down. Lift it up. Do something.

She attempts to help, then recoils.

MOTHER

Phew! They'll know when you get there. Your hair stinks for a start. How long you been wearing those knickers?

BETTY

It's your job to do the washing, not mine.

MOTHER

And you're old enough to look after yourself. I've got my hands full enough.

ACT ONE

BETTY

And so have I. I'm supposed to go to school, when I get there. I do half the cleaning up, and the shopping, and pinching wood, and picking coal, and getting our two off in the mornings. It's me that gets up, not you – and listening to your moans every day. I've had enough of it. What's more, I never ate that loaf, and you knows it. You just wants an excuse to belt into me. You're a mean devil!

Her MOTHER clouts her, and scuffles her out – throwing her coat after her. She bolts the door. BETTY gives it a couple of hefty kicks from outside. Then her footsteps recede.

The MOTHER pants – at first vibrant with victory. Then she subsides at the table. Her shoulders fall and she begins to weep – watched by the silent, appalled BOYS.

Light change.

ACT ONE SCENE THREE

Outside the Honeywell House.

The windows are lit. Happy sounds coming from within. A BOY and GIRL arrive, and are welcomed by MRS HONEYWELL in the doorway. They go in. Pause. TWO GIRLS arrive, and are let into the house. Then a LITTLE GIRL with her MOTHER. All the girls are nicely dressed, with hairbands, gloves, capes, shawls, and their party shoes in their hands. The last woman is a rounded FARMER's WIFE. She kisses her daughter in the open doorway.

FARMER'S WIFE

Be good. Bye bye.

There is a slight movement in the shadows. The FARMER'S WIFE peers into the gloom.

                    FARMER'S WIFE
Who's there? Who's that?

She moves into the road. We can just make out the form of a MAN.

                    FARMER'S WIFE
Is that you, Alf Silver?

The MAN melts away.

                    FARMER'S WIFE
You go on home. We don't want any of your nonsense.
You go on home, or I'll fetch the police after you!

She leaves.

BETTY enters, with hunched shoulders and dragging feet. She reaches the door and hangs about. She makes to pass on, then returns for a look in the lighted window. Her mouth makes an "Ooh" shape. She goes up the steps and lifts her hands to the knocker, but cannot bring herself to touch it. She sits on the step. The MAN in the shadows moves slightly. She jerks up and stares – but sees nothing. She slumps against the door. It opens.

                    MRS HONEYWELL
Hullo. It's Betty! I thought I saw someone at the
window. Come in, my dear. No need to be shy. We've
just started the games ...

BETTY follows her in. The door closes. The MAN approaches. We only see his back as he creeps up to the door, where he stands, framed, and sinister. He sidles along to look in the window. Now, there is something pathetic about him, his hands clutched on the sill, straining to see.

Light change.

ACT ONE

ACT ONE SCENE FOUR

The Party.

A kitchen/living room, which is the quintessence of cosiness.

A fire burns; a black cat purrs on a cosy armchair; a kettle sings on the hob. The room is festooned with paper chains, and there is plenty of holly and mistletoe. The table, laden with jellies, cakes and trifle, is pushed back from its normal, central position, and gets many an admiring glance from the CHILDREN.

BETTY is wearing a new dress, lent by one of the mothers.

A game is just over, and a BOY holds up a parcel in excitement.

BOY

I've got it! I've got it!

He tears open the wrappings, surrounded by NOISY EXCITED CHILDREN. It is a money box in the shape of a red pillar box. There is a fight among the BOYS – and BETTY – for its possession. The THREE WOMEN move in to calm them down.

MRS HONEYWELL

Now children. Now children, I think you'd better all sit down.

MISS BEECH

Sit down everybody. Let's have a little bit of quiet. I think we could have some music, Faith, don't you?

MRS FINCH

Another game in a minute.

MRS BEECH

(*With a greasy smile.*)

What about Phyllis playing us one of her little pieces?

Stifled groans from the CHILDREN. MRS HONEYWELL expands. Her PHYLLIS hangs back coyly.

> MRS BEECH
> 'T'won't do them no harm to bide quiet for a bit.

BETTY gives her a scowl.

> MRS HONEYWELL
> Come on, then, Phyllis. Mr Pooley says she's doing very well.

PHYLLIS sits at the piano and gives an appalling rendition of a small piece by Boccherini. The reprise gets worse and worse, and flounders altogether.

> MRS HONEYWELL
> Very nice, my love. 'Course, that's her new piece.

> MRS BEECH
> She wants more practice.

> MRS FINCH
> It's coming on, Phyllis.

PHYLLIS squirms. BETTY, in the corner, lifts her eyes to heaven.

> MRS FINCH
> I tell you what. Arnie can give us a song.

ARNOLD comes forward, composed, as befits a local chorister and soloist, and sings three verses of "In The Bleak Mid-Winter." The young VICAR enters quietly in the middle of this, and is greeted by MRS HONEYWELL. Applause. BETTY is lost – affected by the singing.

> MRS BEECH
> Cheer up, Betty!

The GROWN-UPS laugh. BETTY is startled, and moves away.

ACT ONE

VICAR

I'm afraid Betty has sensibilities.

MRS HONEYWELL

Oh, she's very sensible, Mr March. Just as well, poor little thing.

VICAR

Yes.

MRS HONEYWELL

Of course, I don't let Phyllis play with her usually. But, well, I felt sorry for the child humping that washing about. I don't suppose she's even been to a *private* party before.

MRS FINCH

We had to lend her a dress, you know.

MRS BEECH

Mothers' Union to the rescue, as usual.

The VICAR blenches. But the CHILDREN surge round wanting another game.

CHILDREN

Let's play Blind Man's Buff! Can we play Blind Man's Buff? Blind Man's Buff!

The VICAR retires with a cup of tea and a large piece of cake.

MRS HONEYWELL fetches a scarf and binds a LITTLE GIRL's eyes. She blunders about amid happy screaming, and grabs a BOY.

LITTLE GIRL

It's Wally!

WALLY is the Blind Man. He grabs a GIRL, and pulls at her curls.

> WALLY
>
> *(Hoarse.)*

Gladys Warchurch!

GLADYS, eyes bound, staggers about ineffectively, but manages to get her arms around ARNOLD, the beau. The way she lifts her head up, she may well be cheating.

> GLADYS
>
> *(Soft)*

Arnie!

Oohs and Aahs.

ARNOLD, eyes bound, is tougher than his sissified suit indicates, and leaps about energetically – a danger to life, limb, and tea table. BETTY, getting boisterous, tries to avoid him.

> ARNOLD
>
> *(Reaching out.)*

I know who it is!

BETTY jerks away. There is a horrible ripping sound, and the dress parts, bodice from skirt – and most of the side-seam – displaying her awful petticoat. A shocked silence. BETTY is too stunned to speak. Then she flees from the room. We hear the front door slam.

> MRS FINCH

She's run off!

> MRS BEECH

That lovely dress!

MRS HONEYWELL exits to the hall, and back again.

> MRS HONEYWELL

Go after her, Win. She's left her coat.

ACT ONE

MRS BEECH

Oh, she'll come back. Whatever will Mrs McNally say?

MRS FINCH

(To the VICAR)

That was all done by hand. I wouldn't have lent it.

MRS BEECH

A decent child would have known better.

VICAR

Ladies ...

But they turn on him, and he wilts.

VICAR

Perhaps if you served the tea now?

The WOMEN respond.

MRS HONEYWELL

(Calls out)

Tea now!

MRS BEECH

(Calls out)

Tea now!

MRS FINCH

(Calls out)

Tea now!

The VICAR assists them in pulling the table to the centre of the room. The CHILDREN are sorted out and seated. Funny hats are put on, crackers are pulled, and mottoes read across the table. Whistles are whistled, while the WOMEN pour lemonade and serve the trifle.

Light change.

BETTY'S WONDERFUL CHRISTMAS

ACT ONE SCENE FIVE

A hill above the town.

BETTY staggers on, in her torn dress, panting heavily, having run herself out. The lights of the town twinkle below her. She sinks down under a tree, rubbing her arms, and groaning against the cold. There is the sharp CRACK of a twig. She jumps to her feet, alert, and listens. All is still.

BETTY

Anybody there? Who is it?

She looks down at her raggedy dress, and groans again.

BETTY

Oh-h ... crumbs! Oh-h crumbs!

She looks around to make sure she's not being followed, then makes her way off. The MAN enters, and crosses, following her.

Light change.

ACT ONE SCENE SIX

In the Woods. Trees and snow.

BETTY enters.

BETTY

Please God, help me. I'm lost. I'm cold!

She stumbles and recovers.

BETTY

I can't go back there. I can't go home. I'll have to go on. Somewhere ...

ACT ONE

She tries to move on, but she is exhausted. She crouches against a tree.

BETTY

Please God ... Please God ... send somebody to help me.

The MAN looms up behind her.

BETTY

(Screams.)

Ahhhhh!

The MAN puts a hand over her mouth. She breaks away.

BETTY

Mr Silver! What's the matter? What do you want?

He grabs at her. She eludes him.

BETTY

Don't! Stop it! What are you doing? Hey! I'll tell my Mum on you!

He throws her down. She screams. There is a violent tussle. She is strong and used to fighting, and almost evades him several times – crying, grunting and calling.

BETTY

Mr Silver! Don't! Please! Please! Help! Mr Silver! Help! Help!

The snow thickens as the tussle becomes grim – punctuated by grunts and gasps. Snowflakes obliterate the scene. The wind gets up and screams ... or, perhaps it is the child.

Light change.

ACT ONE SCENE SEVEN

The same, but different.

Carpets of spring flowers underfoot, and the trees are green. Warm, soft light. Everything glows. A WOMAN steps out of the forest and looks at BETTY, who is lying asleep. This is MRS SPRING-IN-WINTER, who is heavily-built, with a white bun under a bonnet, brown velvet fitted jacket, a sprigged skirt with flounces, and black boots. Her cheeks are rosy.

> MRS SPRING-IN-WINTER
> Wake up. Wake up!

> BETTY
> What?

> MRS SPRING-IN-WINTER
> Do you want a golden guinea, or don't you?

BETTY sits up with a jolt.

> MRS SPRING-IN-WINTER
> That usually does the trick. Let me look at you.
> Hmm ...

BETTY looks down in surprise. She is wearing a neat, brown dress with some orange about it, a shawl, buckled shoes, and her hair is modestly curled about her shoulders. She touches it in amazement.

> BETTY
> Am I asleep?

> MRS SPRING-IN-WINTER
> Certainly not. Have a drink of water.

From nowhere, she produces a silver cup of water.

ACT ONE

MRS SPRING-IN-WINTER

Drink up. Straight from the spring, and as soft as butter.

BETTY

It freezes your teeth.

MRS SPRING-IN-WINTER

Here. Wheat germ, raspberries, crushed oats, and yoghourt. We must get rid of those spots.

She moves about as BETTY crouches, eating obediently, and with relish. Each time she touches a tree, it bursts into bloom. She turns, and regards BETTY's awestruck face.

MRS SPRING-IN-WINTER

There. When you can do that, you'll be grown up. Until then, you're not very interesting. Don't forget that.

BETTY

No, Miss.

MRS SPRING-IN-WINTER

And don't call me Miss. My name is Mrs Spring-in-Winter. Here ... A drop of goat's milk.

She hands BETTY a large snail's shell. BETTY drinks, then makes to lick her dish. She catches MRS SPRING-IN-WINTER's eye, and refrains.

MRS SPRING-IN-WINTER

Have you finished? Good. Now. First lesson. What is The first flower of Spring?

BETTY

(Eager.)

Snowdrop.

MRS SPRING-IN-WINTER

Wrong. Eranthis hyemalis. The winter aconite. Bright as a buttercup. Likes a bit of shade. Don't plant too deep, and try not to disturb. Next...

BETTY

What? Oh... Crocus.

MRS SPRING-IN-WINTER

Well?

BETTY

Then daffodils, tulips, lilac... ah... roses, herbaceous, asters, dahlias, and chysanths.

MRS SPRING-IN-WINTER

Well, at least she knows her seasons. What's your favourite flower, girl?

BETTY

White violets, and primrose.

MRS SPRING-IN-WINTER

What about delphiniums?

BETTY

Too big.

MRS SPRING-IN-WINTER

Lupins?

BETTY

I don't know.

MRS SPRING-IN-WINTER

Precisely. A bank manager's flower. *(Cunning.)* And what about those enormous pink and white striped camellias that grow against the manor wall?

ACT ONE

BETTY

(Defensive and unsure.)

They don't have no scent.

MRS SPRING-IN-WINTER

Hmm. You're fond of saying what you think. Still, she has sensibility.

BETTY

What's that?

MRS SPRING-IN-WINTER

It means that you mustn't waste time feeling sorry for yourself. And don't over-eat. Your sort gets fat and miserable. Remember: fat means miserable, so don't be taken in by jolly jokers. Have you got your book?

BETTY looks. There is a NOTEBOOK and a PENCIL attached to her skirt. She brandishes both triumphantly.

MRS SPRING-IN-WINTER approaches a modest, twiggy plant covered with sweet, waxy, yellow bells.

MRS SPRING-IN-WINTER

Chimonanthus fragrans. Known as the Wintersweet. You must put it in good soil, with a southern aspect, and protect it from the wind. Now, smell!

BETTY leans and smells the chimonanthus. It has a lovely fragrance.

BETTY

Oooh!

MRS SPRING-IN-WINTER

What do you say to that?

BETTY

It's lovely! Sweet – but not so heavy as a lily.

MRS SPRING-IN-WINTER pats her on the head, pleased.

> MRS SPRING-IN-WINTER
> Good. Good. Now, when you get to the palace, you'll be mocked and snubbed. That is, if anyone speaks to you at all. You must expect it.

> BETTY
> The palace?

> MRS SPRING-IN-WINTER
> Remember, people don't like strangers poking in. That's human nature. If you want to join, you must eat what they eat, wear what they wear, be amiable, and wait your turn.

> BETTY
> I'll remember. I'll try, anyway. Sometimes, I . . . speak up.

> MRS SPRING-IN-WINTER
> Yes-es. Well, if anyone makes a joke – laugh.

> BETTY
> Even if I don't think it's funny?

> MRS SPRING-IN-WINTER
> Try not to make a habit of it. But it's only kindness, after all. What's this?

She touches a strange Chinese tree. Its yellow fronds quiver at her touch.

> MRS SPRING-IN-WINTER
> Hamamelis mollis!

> BETTY
> I beg your pardon?

ACT ONE

MRS SPRING-IN-WINTER

Witch-hazel. Make a brew of witch-hazel for the skin. It closes the pores. Never use soap and water on the face. Eat honey, never white sugar, and clean your skin with complexion milk. Once, not twice, or you remove the natural oils. And don't frown.

BETTY is attracted to a clump of large white, open flowers, standing in stiff, dark green leaves.

BETTY

Gosh. What are these?

MRS SPRING-IN-WINTER

Heavens! Doesn't she know a Christmas rose when she sees one? Helleborus niger – slow to flower, heavy soil, manure and leaf mould – plenty of slug bait. Aha!

MRS SPRING-IN-WINTER bends quickly and rises with an enormous glistening SLUG. BETTY screams. The SLUG moans and expires.

MRS SPRING-IN-WINTER

Slugs! Slugs! Tam-sin!

A LARGE THRUSH enters.

MRS SPRING-IN-WINTER

Tam-sin! Quick! Slug. Under my boot.

THRUSH

(with a wonderful trill)
Mrs Spring-in-Winter! *(Fibrillating her wings.)* Too kind. Too kind!

She exits with the slug – bowing.

MRS SPRING-IN-WINTER

Not at all. *(To BETTY)* Pleasant bird. Gets hysterical when nesting. I give her molasses and a touch of iron tonic, otherwise she slides ...

BETTY

Slides?

MRS SPRING-IN-WINTER

She's been known to tip her eggs out of the nest. It's not funny!

BETTY

'Specially if you was walking underneath!

She wilts under MRS SPRING-IN-WINTER's look.

MRS SPRING-IN-WINTER

You do want to grow up, don't you?

BETTY

Oh, yes, yes. At least, I think so. It can't be any worse than ...

MRS SPRING-IN-WINTER

Right. Well, in that case, learn to keep vulgarity for the bedroom. And now, for my heart of hearts ...

The TREES part to reveal a glade of large pink and white blossoms, with a delicate appearance of great beauty.

BETTY

Wow! What are those?

MRS SPRING-IN-WINTER

R-R-Rhododendrons!

ACT ONE

BETTY

Are they? I thought they was for parks. Bright pinks. And red.

MRS SPRING-IN-WINTER

Those are the hybrids. Nasty things for nasty people. You will grow the species.

BETTY

Beg pardon? The what?

MRS SPRING-IN-WINTER

The species! Culled by the brave Robert Forest. By the incomparable Kingdon-Ward from the jungles of Burma – the slopes of Yunnan. The foothills of Szechuan itself!

BETTY

They're lovely. Lovely!

MRS SPRING-IN-WINTER

Here they are, my fragile fortuneis – the gentle Griffithianums, auriculatums, ciliatums, the Loderis...

BETTY

Whoo!

MRS SPRING-IN-WINTER

The white and yellow blossoms from the rain forests. The musky Maddeniis, manipurenses, Edgeworthiis, Lindleyis... Nuttalliis...

BETTY

Gosh!

MRS SPRING-IN-WINTER

The prince's name is Arthur.

BETTY

Arthur?

MRS SPRING-IN-WINTER

Arthur. His mother was staying in Freshwater, on the Isle of Wight. Near the home of Lord Tennyson. The idylls, you know.

BETTY

Is he—? The prince. Is he handsome?

MRS SPRING-IN-WINTER

No. As a matter of fact, he's rather short. But nice grey eyes. And very strong.

BETTY can't hear enough of this fascinating subject.

BETTY

Yes?

MRS SPRING-IN-WINTER

Inclined to asthma.

BETTY

Oh dear.

MRS SPRING-IN-WINTER

When he's crossed.

BETTY

And when he isn't?

MRS SPRING-IN-WINTER

Some sense of humour, and ...

BETTY

Yes?

ACT ONE

MRS SPRING-IN-WINTER

It's unfashionable but, you never know when it may come in handy. He's, ahem, kindly.

BETTY

(A happy smile.)

He's kind?

MRS SPRING-IN-WINTER

Kind.

BETTY

(Sighs, then)

What colour is his hair?

MRS SPRING-IN-WINTER

Mercy me, where's the sun? Look at the time! The pigs will be farrowing, and I'm due at the brick factory. Good grief, girl, I've better things to think about.

BETTY

Not very tall you said?

MRS SPRING-IN-WINTER

Not very.

BETTY

But very strong.

The bushes and flowers begin to sway back and forth.

BETTY

Is he musical?

MRS SPRING-IN-WINTER

He's got a good pair of lungs.

BETTY

Can he swim?

MRS SPRING-IN-WINTER

Like an eel. Now look what you've done!

A soft murmur and MUSIC from the trees.

MRS SPRING-IN-WINTER

Silly things! I can't be concerned with flowers when they get romantic. It always happens when they settle in temperate countries. Do remember to stand nicely.

BETTY

Don't leave me!

MRS SPRING-IN-WINTER

Follow the celandines. Take a bath every day. And don't serve tinned food.

BETTY

But I don't know anything! I shan't be able to manage! Please come back and help me ...

MRS SPRING-IN-WINTER

(Going.)

Listen to the music ...

She exits.

The trees dance. BETTY sways languidly to the music.

BETTY

Oh blow! Just when I was getting started. What did she say? No tinned food. Don't wash your face. Grow rhododendrons. And laugh at all the jokes. And there's celandines everywhere!

ACT ONE

She wanders, seeking a path. The trees move aside for her. She walks along the paths created for her until she reaches a clearing. She is about to sit down to rest, when a long tendrillly ARM moves her away.

LONICERA

Not on me, ducky. I'm Lonicera Fragrantissima. Winter flowering. I shouldn't be here. At all really. I don't know what on earth made me take root!

BETTY

Gosh, you do smell nice!

LONICERA

Thanks. Thank you. You're looking very nice yourself.

BETTY

I look like a robin, don't I?

LONICERA

Not surprising. It's his gear you're wearing.

BETTY

Really?

LONICERA

Well, you used to give him bits of crust at the window. It all comes back to you.

BETTY

He came in the house once or twice, but Mum didn't like the mess he made.

LONICERA

And who called him Turd the Bird?

BETTY

It was only in fun.

LONICERA

Well, he didn't like it. There's nothing wrong with birdlime, you know.

BETTY

I never said there was.

LONICERA

So, where are you off to?

BETTY

The palace, I think.

LONICERA

The palace! Why, what's happening there?

BETTY

I don't really know.

LONICERA

Look, ducky, if you've got ambitions. *(Shakes his head.)* I don't mean to be unkind. I'm not saying you're the ugly duckling – anything like that. Still, I know how all you girls dream about marrying the prince.

BETTY

I never said that.

LONICERA

You just happen to have heard that he's looking for a bride, I suppose.

BETTY

Anyway, somebody told me he wasn't all that good-looking.

ACT ONE

LONICERA

Oh ho – spiteful! Don't you be so rude, Miss. All princes are handsome. The last one had a mouth like a fish-tank. They couldn't wait to fall in!

BETTY laughs, and reels around, bumping into SIR HORSE CHESTNUT, dressed for a day at the races. He is considerably put out, and slashes at her with his crop.

BETTY

(Astonished.)

It's a conker!

CHESTNUT

Sir Horse Chestnut – damn you!

BETTY jumps.

BETTY

There's no need to swear.

He cuts at her again.

BETTY

Hey!

CHESTNUT

Get back there! Whoa!

He walks about, slashing angrily.

LONICERA

I take it we didn't win then.

SIR HORSE CHESTNUT growls.

LONICERA

How did he run? Did he finish? Was it the water jump?

CHESTNUT

Upsides the favourite at the third last – dammit!

LONICERA

(Patiently. He's been here before.)

What happened?

CHESTNUT

Into a hole. Feller lost his whip. Ran down the fence. Made it to the last. Brought down the favourite. Pecked on landing. Blew up on the straight, and parted company.

LONICERA

So, he wasn't even placed?

CHESTNUT

Placed! Placed! The screw finished up in the tea tent with a meat pie in one ear and an Irishman's arithmetic in the other. A laughing stock!

LONICERA

That's torn it.

CHESTNUT

He'll be all right for the cup, y'know. We'll get a better price on him in the antepost.

LONICERA

All very well for you. I'm in rather deep, cocky. On *your* recommendation.

BETTY

Have you been betting?

ACT ONE

LONICERA

Tell you what – why don't you sell the youngster here a decent pony? She'll never make it to the palace without a four-footed friend.

CHESTNUT

And what does she want to go there for?

LONICERA

She's got ambitions.

CHESTNUT

Hah! Take my tip. Stick to the smaller tracks.

BETTY

Why?

CHESTNUT

Why? Why? Because you'll have friends. No whip. No handicapper bent on breaking your heart. Leave the Classic to the big rogues – that's my motto.

LONICERA

He's right you know. Once you leave here, you can't come back.

BETTY

If I get to the palace, I shan't want to.

CHESTNUT

Ha ha. Don't you be so sure. A bird in the hand. Better to be a big fish in a small pond. You know what happens to minnows and tadpoles. They get eaten up. You take my tip: stick to the provinces. Play the second circuits. I know what I'm talking about.

LONICERA

Sell her the horse, cocky.

An ACORN, dressed as a jockey, brings on a sturdy SHETLAND PONY.

> **BETTY**
>
> Oh! He's lovely! *(She puts out a hand.)* Will he bite?
>
> **CHESTNUT**
>
> Bite? Bite? Of course he bites! You bite, don't you? *(To the pony)* Get back there! Whoa! Strong as an ox. Go all day. No vices. Good in traffic. Easy to box. Sound in knee and wind. Never been known to knock.
>
> **BETTY**
>
> What?
>
> **CHESTNUT**
>
> Knock.
>
> **BETTY**
>
> What? Well, does he bite his crib?
>
> **CHESTNUT**
>
> No.
>
> **BETTY**
>
> Suck his wind?
>
> **CHESTNUT**
>
> No.
>
> **BETTY**
>
> Bit injuries?
>
> **CHESTNUT**
>
> No.
>
> **BETTY**
>
> Girth galls, broken knees, sore back, saddle galls, pricked feet, cracked heels, bruised soles –?

ACT ONE

CHESTNUT

No!

BETTY

Any fever in the feet, ringbone, spavin, thrush, sidebone, splints, curls, or thoroughpins?

CHESTNUT

None.

BETTY

No cold in the head?

He shakes his head.

BETTY

Coughing?

CHESTNUT

No

BETTY

Strangles?

CHESTNUT

No.

BETTY

Roaring?

CHESTNUT

Never.

BETTY

Whistling?

LONICERA
(Quickly)

Cross his heart.

                    BETTY

Tubed? Fired? Blistered?

Both shake their heads, sorrowful at her suspicions.

                    BETTY

Sweet itch? Ringworm? Lice?

They continue to shake their heads. BETTY walks around the pony.

                    BETTY

Wingles?

                    BOTH

What's that?

                    BETTY

I made that up.

CHESTNUT follows her.

                    CHESTNUT

Breath as sweet as a chocolate drop.

                    BETTY

But does he kick?

                    CHESTNUT

Kick? Kick? Damn you, of course he kicks! You kick,
don't you? *(To Pony)* Whoa! Get back there!

                    BETTY

I'll have him. What's his name?

                    CHESTNUT

Whitefang. And he'll cost you ...

                    BETTY

Thirty pound. Not a penny more.

ACT ONE

CHESTNUT

Twenty – with tack.

BETTY

Ten, tack and stabling all in.

CHESTNUT

A five-pound note, and a free horsebox to county shows!

BETTY

Done!

BETTY hands over the money in gold coin.

BETTY

He's no bargain.

CHESTNUT

(Chuckling in greedy glee.)

Take my tip. Never buy a cheap horse.

He helps her up on to the pony.

BETTY

Can you tell me the way?

LONICERA

If we knew that we wouldn't be hanging around here, would we?

CHESTNUT

My advice is: take the Ascot road, leave Aintree on your left, avoid Doncaster, skirt round Lingfield, and straight through Plumpton and Goodwood.

LONICERA

And I shouldn't talk to any strange plants.

CHESTNUT

You might get done.

BETTY sets off on the pony, turning to wave goodbye.

BETTY

I'm rather nervous!

LONICERA

(Already distant.)

So you should be. Cheeky thing!

CHESTNUT

Far safer to stay at home. Stay with us!

The stage darkens swiftly, and BETTY threads her way through the dark shapes of the forest. Strange MUSIC. Little fires flicker here and there. A horse whinnies. The MUSIC increases and there is a long, screaming cry. It's hard to say whether it's human or from a beast. Subtle movements in the shadows.

Then, out of the forest, come MEN wearing giant antlers with an enormous spread, and heel-less, doe-skin shoes. They caper rhythmically, swaying their huge antlers, their bodies held back, kicking forward with their feet. The dance increases in intensity, strange rather than menacing, until BETTY is whirled into the centre. She's now wearing a soft white gown and a wreath of leaves and flowers in her hair, which now flows to her waist, soft and fair. She tries to escape, making ritual movements from one MAN in the circle to another. Eventually, at the climax, the MEN crowd in and engulf her, and she is carried up aloft, recumbent, on a cradle of antlers.

Light change.

ACT ONE

ACT ONE SCENE EIGHT

The Kitchen Garden of the Palace.

The old brick walls are covered with espaliered trees, flowering and fruiting. There is a strawberry patch, raspberry canes laden with raspberries, and salads in neat rows.

BETTY enters, composed and beautiful in a white dress, now encircled with gold filigree and pink ribbons. She has two white whippets on a lead. The gardener bows and touches his cap. She nods graciously.

BETTY

Good morning.

GARDENER

Good morning, my lady.

BETTY

What a strange garden!

GARDENER

All in order, I trust, my lady?

BETTY

Oranges, and apples on the same tree. Fruit and flowers together! How do you manage that?

GARDENER

But this is the palace garden, my lady.

BETTY

The palace! Oh, yes of course, I see. Tell me. Why do you call me my lady?

GARDENER

Why, because you are, my lady.

BETTY

How do you know?

GARDENER

Why, because you'm dressed like a lady, and you speaks like a lady, if you please.

BETTY

Oh, do I? Please, what's your name, if I might ask?

GARDENER

Godfrey, my lady.

BETTY

Is that your Christian name?

GARDENER

Surname, my lady.

BETTY

And your first name?

GARDENER

Aaron, Ma'am.

BETTY

Aaron. Aaron Godfrey. Yes, it has a good ring.

GARDENER

Begging your pardon, my lady.

BETTY

Oh, there's no need to do that, Mr Godfrey.

GARDENER

(Shocked.)

Oh, plain Godfrey will do, my lady. Just Godfrey is quite enough.

He seems scared.

ACT ONE

BETTY

If you say so. Don't you want to better yourself?

GODFREY

I hope I know my place, my lady.

BETTY

Oh, all right. Pick me a pear. No, not that one. Higher up. There. Oh, you can reach it, man!

He gets it for her, shining it carefully.

BETTY

Mmm. It's delicious.

GODFREY

Would there be anything else, my lady?

BETTY

No. You'd better be about your business.

He scurries to his work thankfully.

BETTY

I can't believe he really likes being a squit.

She turns away. GODFREY shakes a fist at her back. She turns and catches him. He bends over his work – fast.

BETTY laughs.

BETTY

You had me worried, Godfrey. I'd have slung a dung ball! I'm not sure I like going up in the world.

The LADY SELENA – aristocratic, long-nosed and pale – saunters by, attended by her MAID and TWO FAWNING COURTIERS. One has a hooded falcon on his wrist. She laughs a tinkling laugh, then stops at the sight of BETTY. She looks her up and down. Then, with a faint smile of contempt, she passes on. BETTY curtsies correctly. COURTIER #1 slips her an interested glance.

BETTY

Phew! If looks could kill! This gets worse every
minute.

TWO FOOTMEN, teasing TWO PRETTY MAIDS, jostle by. They are having fun, laughing and squealing. The MAIDS tread on some of the GARDENER's flowers. He glares at them. But at the sight of BETTY, the FOOTMEN and MAIDS look afraid, go silent, bob, and pass quickly on their way. Their squealing starts again offstage.

BETTY

Oh blimey. I'm really nowhere. Perhaps the conker
was right after all. At least in the forest they spoke to
you. Even when they were duffing you up.

GARDENER

(Muttering.)

They don't know their place.

BETTY

I wish I knew mine. Well, goodbye, kitchen garden. I
can't stay here any longer. Lucky for them that can.

She walks off.

Light change.

ACT ONE SCENE NINE

The Palace Terrace.

The palace is very fine. Rococo. There are statues, flowers in urns, groups of COURTIERS, colourfully dressed, making

ACT ONE

witty conversation – some walking about and showing off their fashionable garments.

In a corner, a squat YOUNG MAN plays with gadgets on a table –

TWO MONGRELS at his heels. Enter the PRINCE, playing with a ball and cup. His manner is lordly, benign, and gracious. He is accompanied by the CHANCELLOR, TWO COURTIERS and a PRETTY LADY. Every time he gets the ball in the cup, there is applause. He allows COURTIER #2 to try, and smiles generously when the man muffs it. The PRETTY LADY tries, and is filled with laughing confusion. A mood of gaiety.

Bored, the PRINCE moves away, descending from the terrace to the walk by a broad flight of steps. He pauses to smell a rose. COURTIER #1 immediately plucks it for him, but he passes on with a smile. He circles ceremoniously, followed by the CHANCELLOR, the TWO COURTIERS and the PRETTY LADY, and ascends again – as the others bow to him – and approaches the YOUNG MAN at the table (ARTHUR.)

PRINCE

Fascinating. How are you getting on?

ARTHUR

(Pleased.)

There are some very odd refractions. Would you like to see? If you moderate the wavelengths, like this ...

He dodges around the table.

PRINCE

(Kindly.)

Ye-es, marvellous. Absolutely fascinating.

But he is bored stiff, and moves away. ARTHUR, surprised, returns to his gadgets.

SELINA'S MOTHER, LADY FAY

(Tapping the Prince with her fan.)

Such patience, Sire! The poor little man adores you. And he's such a bore!

PRINCE

(In gentle reproof.)

I suppose so. I just see him as ... innocent.

LADY FAY

Very endearing – in a child.

She moves away gracefully. The PRINCE turns in enquiry to the CHANCELLOR – a wily old bird who is never far from his elbow.

CHANCELLOR

Innocence in a man can be dangerous, Sire.

PRINCE

How so?

CHANCELLOR

An innocent man will give up his life for all sorts of reasons. He is quite prepared to die for a piece of cloth.

PRINCE

Do not all our soldiers rally to the flag?

CHANCELLOR

To the flag, sir. Not to an idea. Ideas breed traitors.

They both look at ARTHUR speculatively. The PRINCE frowns.

PRINCE

(Again, the gentle reproof.)

He *is* my brother.

ACT ONE

CHANCELLOR

(Quietly.)

Half-brother.

LADY FAY joins them smoothly – very Knightsbridge.

LADY FAY

He is so free with everyone. Either he thinks absolutely nothing of himself, to waste his time so – or he is patronising us. I mean, he agrees with everything I say – and I talk absolute rubbish! All I get is a sweet smile. You don't know where you are. The man's an enigma. An enigma!

SELINA approaches, sugar-sweet.

SELINA

Mummy darling ...

She flutters at the PRINCE in a sickly way. He seems to like it.

LADY FAY tickles her under her chin, while looking at the PRINCE to ensure he is watching this tender show of affection.

LADY FAY

Sweetness. There, there ... *(Aside)* Don't worry, my pet. Daddy and Mummy will see to it. Don't forget to look shy. *(To the PRINCE)* How wise of our beloved King to favour the most worthy, the bravest, and wisest of his offspring. How is His Majesty's gout, Sire?

The PRINCE limps a little.

PRINCE

Painful ... painful ...

Gentle laughter from the entourage. SELINA is hoping for the arm of the PRINCE, but he smiles at her, bows, and walks about, giving equal attention to all the LADIES. LADY FAY hops about, with SELINA in tow – trying to show her to advantage.

A MESSENGER enters, and gives the PRINCE a message, bowing.

There is an excited buzz. Everyone looks offstage. The PRINCE arranges his sleeves, and takes a central position to receive the new guest. An idea occurs to him. He takes off his ostrich-feathered hat and gives it to COURTIER #2 who – quick on the uptake – takes his place in the centre, acting the PRINCE. The PRINCE unobtrusively moves to the side. TWO TUMBLING DWARFS enter, followed by BETTY, leading two whippets with golden collars. BETTY is now wearing a train and a gold coronet, and is attended by a plump MAID with ruddy cheeks and dark curly hair. She pauses at the silent, staring group, then bravely drops a deep curtsey.

OLD COURTIER

Charmin.' Charmin.'

The cry is taken up. ARTHUR, from the terrace, looks up from his experiments. He is taken by what he sees, and leans over for a better look.

PSEUDO-PRINCE

Welcome to our fair land.

BETTY

Thank you, sir.

PSEUDO-PRINCE

Do you know who I am?

The COURTIERS crane to witness the joke. BETTY regards him, and then the group. Gently, she disengages the hand of the PSEUDO-PRINCE and is about to curtsey to the PRINCE, when ARTHUR leans over the terrace wall.

ACT ONE

ARTHUR

(Apologetically.)

I'm afraid I'm the Prince.

The crowd turns, annoyed. There is even a subdued hiss. ARTHUR has spoken out of turn. He may be the heir, but he is out of favour and an outsider at court. An angry buzz, and much shrugging of shoulders.

BETTY

(Disbelieving.)

You?

ARTHUR

I'm afraid so, yes.

BETTY

The Prince?

ARTHUR fishes about and finds his coronet on the table. He puts it on over one ear.

ARTHUR

As you can see.

BETTY

Then who's this one?

ARTHUR

Peter – the Bastard. *(Calls down.)* Favourite!

The Court hisses.

BETTY

Well! I don't know what to believe! How tall are you?

ARTHUR

Five ten. No, I tell a lie. I'm five eight and a half.

BETTY

Well, give or take half an inch. Can you swim?

ARTHUR

Like a fish. And I've a good pair of lungs.

BETTY

When you haven't got asthma...

ARTHUR

Oh, I only get that when I'm crossed.

BETTY

(Sighs.)

You're the one. Give me a leg up.

He helps her up the wall. The Court whispers. She looks at ARTHUR expectantly. He clears his throat, nervous.

ARTHUR

(To the Court.)

Ah... Uh... dismiss. You can all go now. That is... clear off the lot of you. I never met such a dozy crew – hanging around all dressed up... Anyone would think it was the Fishmongers' Ball.

They scurry about alarmed – and go – bumping into one another in confusion at the turn of events. The other PRINCE looks rather put out, but his FRIENDS persuade him to leave.

ARTHUR

How was that? Well, they went!

BETTY

It wasn't very princely.

ACT ONE

ARTHUR

No, you're right. But I've never bothered much with all that. It's a bit out of date nowadays. We leave most of it to the Chancellor.

BETTY

I like a man to be his own boss. What's all this?

ARTHUR

Techniques.

BETTY

What are they for?

ARTHUR

I want to improve the lot of my people.

BETTY takes a look, walking around the table. She fiddles with one of the contraptions and gets a slight shock. She jumps and makes a little scream.

BETTY

Hey, that's dangerous! You could hurt people with that!

ARTHUR

Not if it's used properly.

BETTY

What, this little thing?

ARTHUR laughs at her ignorance.

ARTHUR

Oh, that's just a model. The real installation would cover half an acre.

BETTY

Oh. Oh, well, of course, I realised that. I have a mind too, you know.

ARTHUR

Yes, I can see that.

BETTY

It looks like a lot of mischief to me.

A roll of drums. ARTHUR rolls his eyes. More trouble. The QUEEN – extremely grand – in crimson velvet with collar and train, sweeps in with a matter of fact bossiness. She is organizing preparations for the Ball.

QUEEN
(To ARTHUR.)

Ah, there you are.

He kisses her dutifully on the cheek.

The QUEEN'S ATTENDANTS, directed by her imperious arm-waving, begin frantic activity. Wrought iron arbours are fitted together and garlanded with leaves, flowers and ribbons. Swan chairs with silver cushions, little silver tables, elephant seats trimmed with bells, spouting dolphins, a decorated swing, a coconut shy, and a beribboned toffee apple stall are brought on.

BETTY watches, open-mouthed. ARTHUR gets in the way and irritates his mother. The QUEEN pushes aside a CLUMSY WORKMAN and knocks in a nail herself with a competent bang... and bumps into ARTHUR again. TWO WORKMEN remove ARTHUR's table.

ARTHUR

What's all this?

ACT ONE

QUEEN

You haven't forgotten the Ball?

ARTHUR

(He has.)

Oh ... No, no, of course not. More expense! The Goths will get us in the end – that's for sure. Who's on the ramparts?

QUEEN

The Yellow Guard.

ARTHUR

I thought so.

QUEEN

Move aside. Move aside. Now! There must be room for my train!

She takes a turn or two, swishing her train, and comes up against BETTY, who drops a quick curtsey.

QUEEN

Who's this?

ARTHUR

(Very nervous.)

Oh. Ah ... this is the Princess Bettina ... from Lointaine. You know.

THE QUEEN

I certainly *don't* know. Is she on our list?

ARTHUR

Her visit is fortuitous.

THE QUEEN

Don't be pert. What does that mean?

ARTHUR

She's ... ah ... Making a courtesy call. To pay her respects. *(Agitated, to BETTY.)* Have you got a card?

BETTY gives him a very scornful look, turns a sweeping circle, and performs a florid and very low curtsey. Rather cheeky.

QUEEN

Humph! So, I find her all alone. Here. In the garden. With a man!

ARTHUR

No, mother. Only with me. She was on her way to your reception.

QUEEN

(Foghorn)

Unattended?!

The TWO DWARFS tumble on and make deep bows. Their elegant clothes mollify the QUEEN somewhat.

QUEEN

Where did you say she was from?

BETTY

Lointaine, Marm.

The QUEEN ignores her rudely, turning to her son.

ARTHUR

(More and more unnerved.)

Lointaine. You know. Just on the left of Portugalia. Nine hundred leagues in all directions. *(He reads from his notebook.)* Excellent train service, copper mines, iron ore, lacemaking, and very good skiing. Uncle Igor retired there.

ACT ONE

QUEEN

Oh, a tax haven. It sounds very middle class.

ARTHUR

The Princess's father is a Knight of the Vertical Spiral.

QUEEN

(Impressed.)

Oh-h.

She regards BETTY with a speculative stare, lifting her lorgnette, and walking all the way round her.

QUEEN

Most of the Spirals are penniless maniacs. That's common knowledge. I wouldn't say it was an order of substance.

The DWARFS sashay off, returning at once, with sacks and sacks of gold, which they pour out at the QUEEN's feet. She does not flicker, glance, or give any indication that she even sees the DWARFS – let alone the gold. She never looks down. But her manner alters utterly. She extends a gloved hand to BETTY, lifting her from a curtsey.

QUEEN

(Soft as goose-down.)

Stand up, child. Let me see your face. The nose is quite restrained. Royalty must be well-nosed. However, one can go too far. What's this? Hazel eyes?!

She is aghast. All seems to be lost.

ARTHUR

(Hurriedly.)

Spanish royal line. On her mother's side.

                    QUEEN

That would explain it. Annunziata, fetch me my
telescope.

Her lady-in-waiting, ANNUNZIATA, fetches it at the run. The
QUEEN regards BETTY through the telescope. Then snaps it shut
with decision.

                    QUEEN

Ye-es. We-ell ...

                    ARTHUR

Yes?

                    QUEEN
                (Waving him aside.)
Straighten your back, child. Corners of the mouth
turned well up. Remember, a smile suggests approval.
You must learn to be lovable, or they'll cut off your
head. And don't be clever. They'll take a pot at you.
Can you breed?

                    BETTY

I beg your pardon?

ANNUNZIATA whispers in BETTY's ear. BETTY puts her hands to
her face, embarrassed.

                    QUEEN

Speak up, speak up. I'm not deaf.

                    BETTY

I assume so, Your Majesty.

                    QUEEN

Assume ... assume ... that's not Good enough. His
Majesty is looking elsewhere. *(To ARTHUR)* You're
going to be passed over if I don't do something about

ACT ONE

it. We can't just assume. How many sons did your mother have?

BETTY

Three, Marm.

QUEEN

And her mother?

BETTY

Three, Marm.

QUEEN

And your father's mother?

BETTY

(Faint.)

Three, Marm.

QUEEN

Well, I suppose that will do, though it's very repetitive. However, we are used to being bored. Do you swim?

BETTY

Yes, Marm.

QUEEN

Like a fish?

BETTY

Alas no, Marm.

QUEEN

Very proper. Well now, do you like babies?

BETTY

Not very much. That is, I don't really know any.

QUEEN

You will, you will. *(To ARTHUR)* Well, Arthur, I shan't promise anything. I'm a woman of my word. I shall speak to your father. No, don't thank me. Clear the court!

She waves her entourage off, and prepares to follow them.

QUEEN

Well, get on with it, boy!

ARTHUR

Get on with what?

QUEEN

Wooing! You can't expect to breed without wooing. Kiss her! Cuddle! You have my permission.

She gestures to her LADIES-IN-WAITING to scoop up the gold, which they do easily, as it's been poured on to two pieces of cloth, which they pull up the ends of, forming two sacks.

The QUEEN goes.

BETTY watches the LADIES-IN-WAITING exit with the gold, as the DWARFS sit apart, their heads on their knees, snoozing.

BETTY is rigid. ARTHUR plucks up courage and approaches her. He clears his throat.

BETTY

Go away.

ARTHUR

I only wanted to ...

BETTY

Go away!

ACT ONE

ARTHUR

Where to?

BETTY

I don't care! Just buzz off. I've never been so insulted in my life. What a cow!

ARTHUR

Shhh!

BETTY

I don't care if she hears me. She ... she's Vulgar!

ARTHUR

You can't say that about a Queen. She makes the rules!

BETTY

Oh, can't I? I'll say it louder. The Queen is ...

He claps a hand over her mouth. She pulls away, furious. He forgets to let go of her, enjoying the contact.

ARTHUR

We don't want a fuss. I know she's impossible. It's her age. She was a beautiful woman, you know, but she's gone off.

BETTY

I never met such a greedy, bossy ...

ARTHUR

Well, she's fed up. There was the earthquake, and the wheat crop failed, and she doesn't like my face, and my father's an awful twerp ...

BETTY

What did she marry him for then? There's no excuse. All she wants is someone to produce babies. What an insult! I shall end up like her. Somebody's awful mother. Nothing but a bus for little princes and princesses to take a ride in.

ARTHUR

You're very beautiful.

BETTY

And a lot of hard work that took, I don't mind telling you! I haven't had a biscuit or cake in months! Let alone a liquorice allsort, or a toffee, or even a mint humbug!

ARTHUR

(*Fervently.*)

It was worth it. Can I kiss you?

BETTY

No. No, no, no!

ARTHUR

But what *do* you want then?

BETTY

Oh, I don't know. I've come all this way! And for what? It wouldn't be so bad if you were handsome. Look at that brown jacket. You might have spruced yourself up! The fortune-tellers must have warned you I was coming. And all this.

She goes to the table and picks up books and reads the titles.

BETTY

'Sailing in Heavy Weather.' ... Ugh! 'Logarithms.' ... 'Pest Control for Dungeons.' ... 'Deferred Pension Scheme for Senior Courtiers.' ... Honestly! Don't you ever read anything interesting?

ACT ONE

ARTHUR

I once read 'The Lion, the Witch, and the Wardrobe.' And I've read 'War and Peace.'

BETTY

And I suppose, when it comes to art, you're a Philistine.

ARTHUR

I can't say I know what I like, although I certainly know what I don't like. I don't always like what I know, and ...

BETTY groans.

BETTY

Oh, never mind. What about music?

ARTHUR

I do play the flute. And the maraccas.

BETTY

(Softening.)

Do you? Really?

ARTHUR

I like military marches, and trad jazz, and oratorios, and Swinging Suzie Simmons, and Benjamin Britten ...

BETTY

I'm a Dave Brubeck fan myself. Oh, but it's no good.

ARTHUR

Pease let me kiss you.

BETTY

There, you see. Hopeless. I might as well be anybody.

ARTHUR

Oh no. It's you I want.

BETTY

Really? Really and truly? But all those babies! We'd never have any time for any fun. I don't know why I bothered. I'll end up back in the kitchen.

ARTHUR

Not necessarily ...

BETTY

Nappies, prams, mixed feeding.

ARTHUR

Nonsense. We'll hire a nanny.

BETTY

Let someone else look after my children? For money? No. I'll be just a nursemaid – at everyone's beck and call. Me, with a degree! Do you know I read Manners, Languages, Seduction, Astrology, French Cooking, Physics, and three terms of Political and Social Intrigue? All that swotting! And I read Robert Musil – just for the look of it.

ARTHUR

What did you think of him?

BETTY

Fine to begin with, but it all got rather German. You part company.

ARTHUR

That's what I thought! See? We like the same things.

He takes her hands. She pulls them away.

ACT ONE

BETTY

Oh Arthur! It isn't that I want to be mean. I'm very fond of you really. It's just that, well, I've come a long way. It wasn't very nice at home but, well, you knew where you were. There was the shopping, and the errands to do, and the washing to hump. And the Sunday School outings to look forward to. Now, I can do anything – or thought I could. I just wanted to be me for a while. Before ... settling down. I suppose you couldn't ... kill a dragon or something?

ARTHUR

The trouble is I'm rather fond of them. They don't mean to tread on people and set fire to things. What do you say to having a honeymoon on the Costa Brava?

BETTY
(Enraged.)

Oh!!

She picks up a cushion and beats him over the head – chasing him about the stage. Then she bursts into tears and runs off.

MUSIC.

ARTHUR
(Sings.)

From fields and clouds and skies of blue,
From the living forests of the North,
A gentle wind is blowing forth
Both honest and untrue.

It breezes through these gardens fair
And comforts some and worries some,
Undoes and does what can be done,
Brings joy and brings despair.

The skies, some sunny, calm, some rough
Will nourish or destroy with rain
Upon the heads of mad and sane,
Will aid and will rebuff.

Light Change.

ACT ONE SCENE TEN

BETTY is being dressed for the Ball. MAIDS come and go. The QUEEN prowls, supervising. ANNUNZIATA and EVGENIA, both Ladies-in-Waiting, assist.

BETTY
(To the QUEEN.)
What do you think?

QUEEN
Another hairpiece!

TWO MAIDS fix BETTY's hair.

QUEEN
Let me see. Oh, you look like Dusty Springfield. Take it off!

The MAIDS oblige.

QUEEN
Now. Lower the belt. Remember: always present a beautiful line. When you move, people must melt at the sight!

BETTY
(Shaking her head.)
I'll definitely melt in that.

ACT ONE

QUEEN

Quite right. Simplicity is all. Never look foolish. You must always be *inevitable*. The coronet.

BETTY

I've got cold feet.

QUEEN

That's as it should be. I'm always sick myself.

BETTY

You?

QUEEN

Sick as a dog. The penalty of being so sensitive. You've heard of the Princess and the pea?

BETTY

Yes?

QUEEN

Me.

EVGENIA

She could have fooled us.

The QUEEN knocks their heads together. They reel about, staggering.

BETTY

Will I do?

The QUEEN inspects her.

QUEEN

Well, of course, I was lucky. I had an eighteen-inch waist. No matter. Call the trumpeters.

BETTY's entourage forms up around her. She twitches her skirt.

The QUEEN checks the Ladies-in-Waiting.

> QUEEN
>
> Sal volatile, handkerchiefs, two groats for the cloakroom lady, barley sugar ...

ANNUNZIATA offers BETTY a brown paper bag to be sick in. She shakes her head wanly. The TRUMPETERS blare. She moves forward.

> QUEEN
>
> Not yet, not yet ...

The TRUMPETERS blow a prolonged flourish. The entourage moves off.

Light change.

ACT ONE SCENE ELEVEN

The Ball. Fanfare.

BETTY enters. She is greeted by ARTHUR, who presents her to the KING – a nice old boy. The KING and QUEEN take their places, and BETTY, flanked by ARTHUR and PETER, makes a round, to cheers and the popping of champagne bottles. The BAND strikes up a waltz. BETTY looks at ARTHUR expectantly. But he shuffles his feet miserably. The COURT titters. The QUEEN whispers to PETER.

With a flourish, he offers BETTY his arm. They waltz – to general applause. Other COUPLES take to the floor in a fast waltz. Then the floor is cleared, and there are TUMBLERS, SWORD DANCERS and a FLOWER DANCE.

> MAESTRO
>
> The Polka!

ACT ONE

Cries of joy. Everyone takes to the floor, and the gouty old KING even persuades the QUEEN to take a turn – though she makes it plain she thinks it's common. The dance is fast and furious.

As the MUSIC reaches its height, there is a loud EXPLOSION. The lights flicker on and off. Screams, shouts, small arms fire, whines, and bangs. The cry is taken up ...

                ALL

The Goths!!!

DARK MEN in metal and leather pour through the windows, bristling with arms. They stand, massed and ominous.

The screams die away until there is complete silence. Then the Goths, led by their enormous LEADER, leap down with terrifying whoops and yells.

The WOMEN flee. The SOLDIERS, PEASANTS and COURTIERS fight bravely. ARTHUR does his best, but gets clonked on the foot, and hops about in agony. PETER does a lot of expert swordplay. BETTY pushes ARTHUR forward, but he gestures to his bad foot. However, he has another go, and gets clouted again.

Concussed, he reels about. BETTY, incensed, grabs a stout stick and lays about her.

Suddenly, there is a lot of flickering light. The cry is taken up ...

Fire! Fire! Fire!

Noise. The clash of swords. The crackle of burning. The grunts and groans of men fighting.

            END OF ACT ONE

ACT TWO

ACT TWO SCENE ONE

Outside the Palace.

In the background, the palace is burning. PETER and BETTY enter, exhausted. They come across ARTHUR, who gets to his feet wearily.

ARTHUR
Do you think we could have a cup of tea?

They all turn and look at the flames.

ARTHUR
It's the end of everything.

PETER
(Defiantly.)
Nonsense. Long live the King!

A SOLDIER runs on.

SOLDIER
(Kneeling to PETER.)
My lord, the King is dead.

ALL
Dead?

A tired OLD COURTIER enters.

COURTIER
Too much for his poor old heart. Actually, it was the polka that did it.

ACT TWO

ARTHUR

Ah – I'm glad of that.

COURTIERS and SOLDIERS straggle on and the cry is taken up...

The king is dead! Long live the king!

BETTY, PETER AND ARTHUR look at each other. PETER is the hero of the hour. PETER makes to kneel to ARTHUR but he shakes his head.

ARTHUR

No, no. I abdicate. You take it on. It's not in my line.

Sadly, he picks up his cloak and walks off. BETTY makes to follow him, but pauses, and turns to PETER. who holds out his hand, in need. It is PETER's hour of glory. Tousle-haired and torn, he looks wide-eyed and magnificent. BETTY responds to his splendid appearance, and fighting bravery. She takes his hand, amid CHEERS– but watches ARTHUR go, anxious for him.

The CROWD takes up the cry 'Long live the King! Long live the King!' There is cheering... which turns suddenly to a wail of fear and anguish as the CHIEF GOTH leaps down on PETER and engages him in swordplay. The fight is impressive, but PETER is getting the worst of it. The GOTH is more agile, trickier... plays dirty, is less showy. He fights with a fierce, detached glee, unlike PETER, who is earnest in his cause, and stiff-faced with determination not to yield. He looks like he's about to be a dead hero. The lights fade a little, the crowd cringes, and there is a hiss of terror. The GOTH, now toying with PETER, abruptly tires of his fun and contemptuously flicks PETERs sword from his hand and kicks him to the ground in one movement. He lifts his own sword for the kill.

BETTY

(A magnificent shouting growl.)

No!

She throws herself in front of PETER.

GOTH

(Surprised and tired.)

Get out of it. I don't want you.

BETTY

I'm the Princess Bettina from Lointaine. Isn't that worth anything?

GOTH

Are you asking for his life?

BETTY

Name a price. He is our King!

GOTH

Oh, I know that.

He makes to kick her aside and finish his kill. BETTY prostrates herself over PETER's body.

BETTY

You'll have to kill me first!

GOTH

Right.

He lifts his sword in a matter of fact way. BETTY jumps up, aghast.

BETTY

You mean, you would?

PETER staggers to his feet and attempts to restrain her. BETTY shakes him off.

BETTY

(To the GOTH)

You rotten savage! You animal!

ACT TWO

She cuffs the GOTH about the head. He laughs and dodges back. She goes for him again. He lifts her easily with one hand.

BETTY

Put me down! Put me down! My petticoat's showing!

PETER gestures, mouthing instructions. FIVE TOWNSFOLK creep on, above, with a LARGE NET. The GOTH laughs, twirling BETTY around – who screeches. Then he puts her down, and laughs at her giddiness.

GOTH

Princess!

BETTY

I'm not only a princess, I'm a peasant! So, *shut up*!

GOTH

Well, whatever you are, there's a bit of fight in you.

BETTY

And that's all you care about, isn't it? Fighting!

GOTH

What do you expect? I'm a man!

BETTY

Yes! And you've destroyed this lovely palace!

GOTH

It was rotten. And the people in it.

BETTY

Are you so much better? To destroy an ancient and beautiful place? I've heard you lot live in mud huts.

GOTH

(Grasps her by the wrist.)

Little princess peasant – there's more to life than stone masonry. Stop a man from fighting and you'll find there are worse fates than dying by the sword.

BETTY

What's worse than being killed?

GOTH

Living sometimes. You left home, didn't you?

BETTY

Only by accident. By a twist of fortune.

GOTH

Going to stick it out, were you?

BETTY

I didn't say that. Who are you?

GOTH

You can see who I am.

BETTY

(Approaching him.)

Do I know you?

The GOTH lifts his visor.

GOTH

(Sheathing his sword.)

You know me well enough! But, since you have the courage, my fierce princess peasant, I'll wet my sword elsewhere.

He turns to make off, and the NET drops. He struggles, caught like a fish. But his strength is tremendous, and he bursts the cords with ease – to the awed groans of the crowd.

ACT TWO

GOTH

Even your nets are rotten! We'll fashion a few new ropes for you!

He turns – embraces BETTY insolently with one arm, and goes. Angry, BETTY runs to a SOLDIER and grabs a blunderbuss. She aims and fires. There is a puff of smoke, and the gun falls to bits.

BETTY

Oh Blimey.

PETER

I say ... thanks awfully for what you did.

BETTY

That's all right.

He takes her hand.

PETER

What a monster. You saved my life.

BETTY

It's going to be a very tough struggle.

PETER

Don't you worry. We'll win through.

He lifts his sword and the people cheer. He looks noble and gallant.

PETER

I say, did you notice my double-handed back-swing? It had him worried!

BETTY

We need tanks.

PETER

Don't worry, the winter's coming. How will he feed his army?

Light change.

ACT TWO SCENE TWO

White tents on a slope. Here and there, stretchers with WOUNDED SOLDIERS. WOMEN move about, tending to the WOUNDED. PETER, in in simple army clothes, strides on and consults with his officers. BETTY, dressed a nurse, emerges from a tent. The SOLDIERS bow.

CAPTAIN

What news, Your Majesty?

PETER

The town and palace are burnt out. But we have retaken Obrisk.

BETTY

And reinforcements?

PETER

On the way. How are the wounded?

BETTY

Recovering.

PETER

And the cholera?

BETTY

No more fresh cases. Our new laws are taking effect. All we need is food!

ACT TWO

MAJOR

Yes, Sire. We are in a bad way.

PETER

Food. Food! There must be some way!

A MESSENGER enters and gives PETER a letter. He reads it, then throws it down impatiently.

BETTY

Arthur again?

PETER

Some potty idea about making soup out of grass. I wish he wouldn't waste my time.

BETTY

I suppose he's trying to help.

PETER turns away. BETTY sighs. Then she brightens as an OLD MAN, helped by a BOY, pushes on a CART. But, when she looks inside, there is only one sack of grain.

BETTY

Is this all you can find?

OLD MAN

There bain't nothing, Ma'am. Nothing. The fields is all burnt.

BOY

By the Goths!

OLD MAN

The granaries is burnt. The peas and beans and potatoes is all took away. The apple stores is kicked down and trod over. The sugar beets all ate up. People is scratchin' for whatsoever they can find.

BOY

What are we going to do, missus?

BETTY

Don't you worry. We'll survive. What about the beasts?

OLD MAN

Not a cow, not a sheep, not a pig to be found. They've driven them all off.

BETTY

No fowls?

OLD MAN

Not a chick, nor a duck, nary a goose to be seen.

The NURSES, WOUNDED, SOLDIERS and PEASANTS draw near.

NURSE

We shall all starve!

WOUNDED MAN

Famine!

PEASANT

What shall we do? What shall we do?

SOLDIER

Give us food!

PEASANT #2

Save us! Save us!

BETTY jumps on to a munitions case, and shouts above the growing clamour.

BETTY

Shame on you! Do you think King Peter and I will let you starve? Where's your spirit? You deserve to peg

ACT TWO

out, the lot of you! I never met such a lot of cry-babies
in all my life! Are you all in the Sahara Desert?
The Kalahari? Above the snows of Chimborazo, or
Kilimanjaro? Are you marooned at the South Pole?

The CROWD murmurs 'No' – obediently.

BETTY

Where are your wits? Haven't you ever lived rough
before? You don't know what it's all about! Captain,
send a platoon to the rivers. And tell them not to come
back until their knapsacks are full of fish! Tell your
sharp-shooters to bring down the birds of the air.
We'll eat thrush pie for supper. Shoot badger, boar,
deer and wildfowl. Trap moles and hedgehogs. Even
rats if we must!

CAPTAIN

Right, Ma'am.

He and the SOLDIERS make off at the double.

BETTY

(To the OLD MAN.)

Organise the village women to gather nettles, and
sorrel, and dandelion. Look for wood strawberries,
wild raspberries, blackberries, mushrooms, and nuts.
Search for pigeon's eggs, watercress, grass snakes,
and snails. We'll not starve yet!

The stage slowly darkens.

ACT TWO SCENE THREE

White tents on a slope. A wind howls

PETER enters, in a ragged greatcoat. On the other side of the stage, a sorry troop of SOLDIERS, some of them on crutches, hobble on, shivering. PETER inspects the troop. A wolf howls. BETTY enters, in rags and an old shawl. She sinks down. PETER approaches.

PETER

(Furtive manner.)

Any luck?

BETTY

I bargained a pair of boots for an old ham-bone, and I took a cabbage from an allotment. To tell you the truth, I stole it. I nearly got my head shot off.

They share the cabbage, and eat it hungrily. Then PETER gnaws the bone.

PETER

What are we going to do?

BETTY

I don't know. I don't know. Isn't it silly? I used to think that, if you tried hard enough, you must succeed. But we've tried everything!

PETER

Our people are dying. We have failed them. If only I'd had reinforcements. I could have driven out the Goths in a week.

The stage slowly lightens.

BETTY

Instead, they've eaten everything and pushed off. *(Slight pause.)* Have you heard from Arthur?

PETER

Not since he took to the forest.

ACT TWO

BETTY

Probably tripped over a root and broke his neck.
(She sighs.) I wish I were home. Even my Mum's rice pudding was better than this. And I haven't got her to blame now. We're in charge.

Shouts offstage. A FRIAR bursts on, followed by PEASANTS.

PETER

What is it?

FRIAR

A troop, Your Majesty. Marching towards us, with machinery!

BETTY

Armed?

FRIAR

No, my Lady. With food!

The cry goes up.

Food! Food! Food!

The TROOP marches on with loaves of bread and a cauldron. ARTHUR, limping, brings up the rear. The PEASANTS put down the cauldron and start feeding people with bread and soup.

BETTY

Arthur!!

ARTHUR

Betty! Come and have a taste!

He gives her a piece of bread, which she tears at.

BETTY

What have you done to your foot?

ARTHUR

Oh, it's nothing. I tripped over a root. Nearly broke my neck. Here ...

He offers her a bowl.

BETTY

What is it?

ARTHUR

Don't ask, or you won't eat it. It's very good.

BETTY

Mmmm! Delicious!

ARTHUR

That's synthetic bread. Guaranteed to make your teeth fall out. I'm only joking!

PETER approaches, eating bread. He slaps ARTHUR on the back.

PETER

Well I'm damned! Good man!

ARTHUR hunches his shoulders.

ARTHUR

I wish you wouldn't do that.

PETER

No offence, old chap. I'm jolly glad to see you.

ARTHUR

We've been working night and day. I've got my little factory all set up, and we're building a sub-section down by the old railway. Oh, by the way, I hope you don't mind, but I swopped the Winter Palace for a supply of seed grain and second-hand boots.

ACT TWO

PETER

Look here, you'd better be Food Minister.

ARTHUR

Done. *(To BETTY.)* Can you can?

BETTY

I don't know about can. I can bottle. And I can salt beans and smoke pork, and store potatoes and dry apple rings. Try me.

ARTHUR

I'll have her as my assistant.

PETER

We'll discuss it.

They are pushed aside by ARTHUR's PEASANTS who remove the tents and set up their CANNING FACTORY. They erect a wondrous machine and pour in baskets of fruit, and a silver liquid (for the tins) at one end. With a cough, crack, hiccup, grind, whoosh, bleep and click, the other end of the machine produces large cans – one after the other – labelled 'Beans,' 'Plums,' 'Cake,' and 'Chocs.' BETTY kisses ARTHUR, which much affects him.

ARTHUR

(To PETER.)

Don't worry. You can still be king.

PETER

Oh. Thanks.

ARTHUR

I hear you two are thinking of getting wed. I want to wish you both the best of luck.

He shakes hands with them both. There is a solemn moment, then PETER moves away to organise things. BETTY looks at ARTHUR. She feels awkward. He squeezes her hand.

ARTHUR
You'll be queen. You'll be jolly good at it.

BETTY
What about you?

ARTHUR
Me?

BETTY
What are you going to do?

ARTHUR
I thought of getting a little place on the by-pass. Set up a workshop.

BETTY
What for?

ARTHUR
Oh ... ice-creams ... buckets and spades ... I'd like to get into the tourist trade. At least it's peaceful.

BETTY
Perhaps you're right. Except the Goths will probably come and take it off us.

ARTHUR
Not if we keep it small. You know – holiday camps and things. Nothing too glorious. We could specialise in honey – something like that. Just so long as we balance the books and keep everything well insured.

ACT TWO

BETTY

(Teasing him.)

And the doors locked, and the dog licences kept up to date. *(Regrets teasing him.)* I'm sorry, Artie dear. I'm sure you're right. Yes.

They look at each other.

ARTHUR

It's funny, isn't it? If it weren't for the Goths, we'd be married.

BETTY

Have you ... Have you got a girl?

ARTHUR

A girl?

BETTY

A girlfriend.

ARTHUR

You know I haven't. I love you.

BETTY

I was afraid you'd say that.

PETER hammers at one of the big tin cans, trying to open it.

ARTHUR

I hope you don't mind.

BETTY

Of course, I mind. *(Calls.)* Peter, could you shut up making that row?

PETER

Sorry old thing!

BETTY'S WONDERFUL CHRISTMAS

BETTY

I wish he wouldn't call me that.

ARTHUR

Old thing?

BETTY

Quite often, he calls me old girl. He's not as romantic as he looks.

ARTHUR

Still – you'll have very handsome children.

BETTY

Looks aren't everything.

MUSIC. She sings:

> I once thought that felicity
> Was an easy thing to learn to know.
> What became of simplicity?
> Where did this complication grow?

> Nothing stays where it is placed,
> Nothing with perfection's graced.
> How can life be so unfaithful;
> So distastefully deceiving?
> The genuine and honest course
> That I bethought sincerely dealing
> With the basis of existence
> In confusion fast is wheeling.
> Nothing absolute remaining,
> Nothing still or permanent enough
> To take believing.

> Being fair and open-feeling,
> Ever gentle, ever smiling,

ACT TWO

Never was before concealing,
Never was before beguiling.

Clear and helpful, not exacting,
Held in living's ceaseless flow,
Then some sudden germ's infecting,
When did this complication grow?

ARTHUR

I suppose you'll be planning the wedding soon.

BETTY

What you were saying about holiday camps ... It's a great idea! Holiday camps! It might be the answer. Make everybody happy. What do you think?

ARTHUR

Why not? I hope you'll ask me to be your best man.

BETTY

Of course. We could have fairs, and rallies. Zoos and parades. Beauty contests and football matches, and swimming galas! Festivals, carnivals, regattas ... We could even have masked balls!

ARTHUR

Don't forget the cost.

BETTY

Ohh. We'll do cut-price for wagon-loads. All-in rates. Free boar hunting and hunt the slipper. Roseleaf pillows and queen bee jelly for the ladies. Archery for the men; community singing in the throne room, and bangers and mash in the barn! Are you on?

ARTHUR

What? Are you serious? I don't know. I think we could ... think about it.

BETTY

Yowee! *(Turns and calls.)* Peter! Peter! Arthur's got a good idea!

PETER

Hang on.

PETER approaches carrying a large RED BOOK.

PETER

I say, Arthur. Is this yours?

ARTHUR

Oh, yes. I was using it to prop up the spifflicator.

PETER

It's jolly good.

BETTY

Peter, don't tell me you're actually reading a book?

PETER

Don't you be so sarky! It's jolly good. I don't have much time for reading, old chap – all this organizing and fighting and stuff ...

BETTY

What's it called?

PETER

(Reads out.)

Red China's New Deal. Do you think there's anything in it?

ACT TWO

BETTY

Let me see. (*Examines the book.*) No-o.

She throws the book away.

BETTY

What we want is small countries. Not big ones. Big ones are too big. Come and listen to Arthur's idea. If it works, we can have white ponies again, and fur muffs, and maypoles, and Tiptrees Little Scarlet jam for tea!

They go off in a huddle.

Fade to black.

ACT TWO SCENE FOUR

The Holiday Camp and the Beach.

A sunny day. Blue sky. The tents are now trimmed with stripes and scallops. FOUR PARENTS and their SIX CHILDREN are on the beach. The men have their trousers rolled up. The women have their blouses tucked into their knickers and wear big sun hats. TWO of the CHILDREN are shrimping with shrimping nets. The other FOUR CHILDREN are making sandcastles, and so is an OLD MAN.

TWO REDCOATS (a man and a woman) are giving assistance, and handing out flags and balloons. A PIG is roasting on a spit in the background. Enter A MAN IN A SUIT and a WELL-DRESSED LADY, in a long, floral dress. They nod to the PARENTS who gather round as the two new arrivals judge the sandcastles. The REDCOATS approach. One of them carries a beach bag. The MAN IN A SUIT and the WELL-DRESSED LADY confer, then select BOY #1 and the OLD

MAN as the winners. The FEMALE REDCOAT takes prizes out of the beach bag held by the MALE REDCOAT and gives them to the WELL-DRESSED LADY who gives them, smiling, to the winners. Applause.

The REDCOATS then bring on tables and chairs, trimmed with flowers, for the wedding. The holidaymakers roll down their trousers, put on their best hats, and put flowers in the CHILDREN's hair. The TOWN BAND arrives, and begins to tune up. The OLD QUEEN enters, comely in prune satin, attended by SELINA and SELINA's MOTHER.

ARTHUR arrives, and SELINA's MOTHER pushes SELINA unwillingly towards him.

QUEEN

Of course, it's all farcical. Farcical – compared to the old days! Where is beauty? Where is romance?

The QUEEN'S DAUGHTER – rather plain – enters clumpily.

QUEEN'S DAUGHTER

Oh, do shut up, mother!

QUEEN

I'm only glad your father isn't here to see Peter married in a Holiday Camp! Ugh! He liked style, did Hortibrand! Why, when I lost my slipper in the ballroom, he picked it up, and took it to the head gardener.

ARTHUR

Whatever for?

QUEEN

"Take this slipper ... Take this slipper," he said, "and grow a violet in it. When it blooms, I shall find my love again."

ACT TWO

WELL-DRESSED LADY
(Agog.)

And did he?

QUEEN

You may be sure of that. My mother was down at Covent Garden the next morning. We didn't leave things to chance in those days. Matters were properly arranged. And we were all the better for it. You knew where you were. What's more, you knew *who* you were. Not that I've anything against Bettina. Although I did have to tell her, the other day, that a lady wears hooks and eyes, *not* zips.

PETER appears, leading BETTY. They both look radiant.

QUEEN

Ahhh!

Oohs and Ahhs. A jolly PRELATE comes on. Everyone falls silent, ready for the ceremony. PETER and BETTY step forward, flanked by ARTHUR. BETTY looks at ARTHUR.

BETTY

Oh. Ah. Just a mo. I forgot my hankie.

She runs off. Everyone is surprised. The people murmur. There is a pause. People turn their heads. At last, BETTY returns.

BETTY
(Quietly.)

There's a dragon in the dairy.

QUEEN
(Screeches.)

What?!

> PETER

Dragons!

> ARTHUR

Don't panic everyone. Women and children down to the river!

PETER blows a whistle, then starts to hurry off.

> PETER
> *(To BETTY.)*

Awfully sorry about this, sweetie. Will you sound the alarm?

Confusion. All run off, leaving BETTY, who hits a BIG GONG a few times. She puts down the hammer.

> BETTY

Well, I *think* I saw a dragon. I could have been mistaken. He was in among the trees. It could have been a horse jumping a gate. Or boys scrumping apples. Of course, it might be a dragon. It jolly well could be a dragon. I had to speak up. Oh, Arthur! How did I know you were going to look so nice in that blue suit? I mean, not that he looks like a hero. A man can look like a hero and be a bit of an old auntie underneath. Nothing wrong with that. I've got some very nice aunties. Can you hear me, Auntie May?

The DRAGON enters behind her and snorts. BETTY reacts before turning around.

> BETTY
> *(Screams.)*

Dragons!

She jumps on a table, and lifts her skirts up.

ACT TWO

BETTY

Quick! Somebody quick! Dragons!

The GOTH CAPTAIN walks on quietly, and leans on his sword, He watches her wit sardonic amusement. The DRAGON turns away from BETTY and begins wrecking the place. BETTY jumps down, picks up a stick, and waves it at the DRAGON.

BETTY

Gggrrrh on! Get out of it! Buzz off, you great dozy thing! Get your feet out of it! Gggrr!

She turns to the audience.

BETTY

It's no good being frightened of them. If you are, they bite your head off. Just go gggrrr. Like this ...
Gggrrrrh!

This makes the DRAGON jump.

DRAGON

(A soppy wail.)

Stop i-it!

BETTY

See?

But the DRAGON honks, rushes at her, knocking away chairs and tables, and pins her to the ground.

BETTY

Yoo!

DRAGON

Ooh. What a nice head. I'll just bite this off.

But the GOTH leaps in, wielding his sword, and drives off the DRAGON. The DRAGON rolls over.

DRAGON

Pax ... Pax!

The GOTH makes to kill the DRAGON.

BETTY

No! No, don't!

The GOTH turns on her with a nasty smile.

GOTH

(Almost a purring voice.)

And why not this time?

BETTY

How can you? He's meaningless!

GOTH

All the more reason.

He turns to kill the whimpering DRAGON. BETTY leaps forward.

BETTY

Don't!

GOTH

Why not?

BETTY

I have a stupid soft heart and I'm a fool.

GOTH

You are a fool.

But he sheaths his sword and approaches her. He kisses her fiercely, then releases her abruptly so that she stumbles.

BETTY

I'd rather you hadn't done that.

ACT TWO

GOTH

You won't see me again. This is a tame country.

BETTY

You're really going for good?

He nods.

BETTY

I'm sorry. But I'm glad. We're better without you. All that fighting and looting and burning. There must be a better way of living. Why did you kiss me?

GOTH

Part of the same thing.

BETTY

Oh no, it's not. Peter and Arthur don't kiss me like that. They're kind, and thoughtful. They're civilised. They behave like human beings.

The GOTH produces a long wolf whistle. His SOLDIERS – shadowy – appear in the background.

BETTY

Not like that.

He grabs her wrist.

BETTY

I don't like it. I don't want it.

GOTH

You will.

BETTY

Never. I'll never want that.

GOTH

Want. Want! It's all want!

He comes close.

>   GOTH
>
> It's not what you want but what you are!

He turns and thwacks the DRAGON, who honks in pain and fright.

>   GOTH
>
> He'll know me again. And so will you.

The GOTH CAPTAIN leaves swiftly, and his SOLDIERS with him.

BETTY pats the DRAGON, who is wailing plaintively.

>   BETTY
>
> Sssh ... Never mind. We got rid of them before, and
> we'll do it again, if they start any trouble. There,
> they've gone. Don't keep trembling. I'll get you some
> milk.

She finds a jug among the smashed-up furniture, fills a bowl with milk, and give it to the DRAGON, who has a sloshy drink.

>   DRAGON
>
> I'm sorry I tried to bite your head off. I get a touch of
> gall bladder trouble. It makes me irritable.

>   BETTY
>
> You should stick to a bland diet. Nice, smooth river
> weed. Wild garlic. And *no* humans. Steady on with the
> milk.

>   DRAGON
>
> Thanks very much. You're a saint. If there's anything
> I can do for you, you've only to ask. If I can make
> myself useful in any way. Any way at all ...

SMOKE is coming out of the DRAGON's nostrils.

ACT TWO

BETTY

Watch it! Or you'll scorch my dress!

The DRAGON droops his head.

DRAGON

It's always the same. I'm not wanted.

BETTY

Don't take on. Poor dragon. It must be very trying not being invited anywhere.

The DRAGON starts blubbing.

BETTY

Oh, please don't cry. Ohh ... you're making *me* cry.

They both cry.

DRAGON

If only I could do something to help. *(Blubbers.)* If I could help somebody ...

BETTY

Listen. I think they're coming back! Oh, what shall I do? I haven't made my mind up. I think I'm making a mistake! What shall I do? Where can I go?

DRAGON

At last. Oh fortune! At last I can be of help to someone! Hop on my back, princess!

BETTY

But where can we go?

DRAGON

To the forest!

Fade to black.

ACT TWO SCENE FIVE

The Forest.

The DRAGON and BETTY on the move.

>BETTY
>
>*(Sleepy.)*
>
>Gosh. We've been going for ages. Do you know where we are?

The DRAGON gives a merry laugh that conveys that he is hopelessly lost.

>DRAGON
>
>Yes! I'm often down this way. Don't you worry!

Fade to black.

ACT TWO SCENE SEVEN

In the Forest.

BETTY wanders on, alone.

>BETTY
>
>Hey, dragon! Dragon! Where are you? What a clot! Why couldn't he look where was going? Swept off by a sycamore branch. I could have broken my leg. I bet he thinks I'm still on his back! And I don't know which way to go! I mean, how can you? You only know the way you've come. And you're not always sure of that! Oh dear. But I'm not worried. Peter will come and look for me. He's good at things like that. He'll organise a search. Dear Peter. He's so handsome and brave. The

ACT TWO

trouble is he's always brave. Sometimes, it's better
to take to your heels. He'll cop it one of these days.
He means well. Of course, he's a bit vain. I think I'll
have to marry Arthur. I feel more at home with him
somehow. He's more my kind. Not so showy. He'll
make a jolly nice Dad – and look after us all – and
never a cross word. What more could I want? How can
I be so discontented with *two* princes to choose from?
I'll marry dear old Arthur. Peter can have Selina.
She's more his style. All that dressing up and going
out to restaurants. Yes, that's what I'll do. After all,
I am grown up. You have to grow up. I'm grown up. I
must be. I have to be. I'm not!

She slumps against a tree, chin in hand.

BETTY

But what's going to happen? I'm an outcast. I don't
fit in nowhere. Perhaps it's my poor background.
Everybody else seems to fit in all right. *(She groans.)*
It isn't as if I haven't worked at it. I really have tried
to be a grown-up! And if I don't get married soon, me
bloom will wear off. I'll end up an old maid!

Enter LONICERA, swishing in, trailing a lot of fronds.

LONICERA

I suppose what you want, you greedy thing, is Peter's
looks and style, and Arty's homely habits. Pete being
all brave and king-like, and Arty pouring out the old
Teasmade.

BETTY

It does look that way, doesn't it? What are you doing
here?

LONICERA

Vandalism, dear. I was *uprooted.* No string, straw, or sacking. Thrown in the back of a blue two-tone and hurtled fifty miles to add a bit of quaint to a weekend conversion.

BETTY

What happened? Did you die?

LONICERA

Excuse me? Who ever heard of being haunted by the ghost of a shrub? No, fortunately, a passing cow to took a fancy to my best tendril. Ooh! *(He rubs a sore hip.)* One heave and I was away in the wind. Well, they hadn't thought to stake me, or tread me in. It's a wonder I didn't snap off at the base and make a lot of secondary, non-flowering growth. It would have served them right.

BETTY

Well, stand still. I'd better plant you.

LONICERA

Not yet. I might as well take a look round. I'm fussy about company. Well, you're stuck with them when you settle, aren't you?

BETTY

(With feeling)

Yes, you are.

LONICERA

Mind you, if I really take against them, I kill them with kindness.

He gives her a tight, tendrillly hug.

ACT TWO

BETTY

Ooof! Hey!

She moves away and her head droops.

LONICERA

Homesick?

BETTY

Yes, I am. I'd like to see my greedy little brothers – and the copper, steaming, full of washing. And the old lav with the woodlice crawling up the wall, and a big cabbage rose you could look at when you was sitting there. I even miss her yell. And the old oak pews in the chapel, and Sunday School outings, and the smell from the bakery, and the milk-sheds with the cow's breath on you, and kingcups in the marsh. If only you could go backwards. But I can't, can I?

LONICERA

No, you can't. So, you'll have to go forwards. Get a move on!

BETTY

All very well for you. I need something better than that rotten little pony you and the old conker sold me. He bucked me off at the first water-meadow. Anyway, I don't know which way to go.

LONICERA
(Meaningfully)

Don't you?

There is a whine of wind. The LONICERA is blown across the Stage, tendrils flapping.

LONICERA

Whoops. The wind's getting up.

BETTY

What do you mean – don't I?

LONICERA

Don't you? Don't you know what you want? Don't you?

BETTY

Of course I don't. If I did, it would be easy.

But LONICERA is gone. The Stage darkens, and the trees move in menacingly. The MEN WITH HORNS enter, skipping silently. BETTY stands still. They circle around her, to faint rhythmic music.

BETTY

I thought you'd be back. I've expected you. Now you must give me an answer.

She throws up her arms and begins to sway to the music. The dance begins to increase in pace until it is fast and threatening.

BETTY is thrown from one group to another. Then the Dancers form a phalanx of horns against her. She is alone, panting. The men advance with a slow stamping step. When they are almost upon her, she throws out a hand to stay them.

BETTY

(Very loud.)

All right! All right! All right! Damn you! All ... right!!

The MEN fall away. In their midst is the GOTH CAPTAIN.

He stands before her, dark and menacing. Slowly, the men melt away and become the trees.

BETTY

I was afraid I might see you again.

ACT TWO

GOTH
(Easy.)
Were you?

BETTY
But I thought – I hoped – that, if I did, you might not notice me.

GOTH
Did you?

BETTY
I still can't... How can you? It's very hard to take! I don't want you.

GOTH
In that case ...

With a sarcastic smile, he hands her a large, long knife.

GOTH
Kill me.

She draws back.

GOTH
Kill me.

He forces her to take the knife. She steps back, then approaches him. She makes a move to strike, but withdraws. He offers himself to her. She makes to strike. But can't do it. After a momentary hesitation, she throws the knife away, and sinks at his feet.

BETTY
(With a long, drawn-out groan.)
Ohhh! I can't do it!

He stands over her with a triumphant smile. Then he backs away. She slithers to his feet again, and holds him by the legs. He stands, smiling down at her. They stand very still.

Fade to black.

ACT TWO SCENE EIGHT

The Forest. Snow falling.

ALF SILVER blunders to his feet, and stumbles off. BETTY rises, in her old petticoat. She takes a step, winces in pain, then gently lowers herself to the ground, where she sits, in a daze. A long pause. There are cries off.

A BOY runs on, followed by TWO VILLAGERS, the VILLAGE POLICEMAN, MAJOR FOSTER, and BETTY's MOTHER, wrapped in an old shawl.

BOY
I've found her! Here she is! I've found her!

MAJOR FOSTER
Are you all right, child?

WOMAN VILLAGER
She'm safe. Here she be – poor little mite.

She wraps BETTY in a shawl. BETTY starts weeping.

MOTHER
Where is she? There you are! I've been sick with worry. You'll catch your death of cold.

ACT TWO

POLICEMAN

Now, Betty. There's no need to upset yourself. There's something I need to ask you. Has anybody... interfered with you?

BETTY looks at him, and wipes away her tears. There is silence. They all wait for her to answer.

BETTY

(At last.)

No. I'm old enough to look after myself. I got lost.

WOMAN VILLAGER

That child should be in a home. She's neglected.

POLICEMAN

How would you like that, Betty? Your poor mother's got more than she can manage, you know. Matron up at the orphanage would like a nice girl like you. You'd have a comfortable bed, with lots of other girls, plenty to eat. New boots...

BETTY looks at her MOTHER, who simply pulls her shawl tighter.

BETTY

(To MOTHER.)

Do you want me to go?

MOTHER

You must make up your own mind.

BETTY is aghast. Her courage falters.

MAJOR FOSTER

You can't put this poor child in a home. You'll break her heart.

He kneels down before BETTY.

BETTY'S WONDERFUL CHRISTMAS

> MAJOR FOSTER
>
> I could talk to her Ladyship. I know she likes you. She has told me so. Her sons have grown up. Her husband is dead. Come to the manor with me. We can talk to her. If she takes you, you could have a room to yourself, with sprigged wallpaper, and plenty of books; a velvet dress on Sundays, and chocolate eclairs for tea.

Oohs and ahhs from the VILLAGERS.

> MAJOR FOSTER
>
> What do you say?

BETTY looks at her MOTHER, who remains silent.

> POLICEMAN
>
> What do you say, Betty?

A pause. Again, they wait for BETTY's answer. She gets up.

> BETTY
>
> *(To her mother – hoarse.)*
>
> I want to go home.

Her MOTHER puts out her arms and hugs her fiercely. She glares round at the crowd, as she and BETTY turn to go. The others watch her. BETTY stumbles, and her MOTHER gives her an irritable push.

> MOTHER
>
> Pick your feet up! I never met such a clumsy creature.

> BETTY
>
> *(Smiling to the others.)*
>
> I'm home! Happy Christmas!

Fade to black.

THE END

THE SOCIALISTS

Karl Marx

For Buzz Goodbody

THE SOCIALISTS

CHARACTERS

MOIRA, early 40s.
SHOP ASSISTANT
TOBY, teens, dark, pudding hair-cut.
CLAIRE, teens, blonde and attractive.
NICK, teens, stocky, Jewish.
PAUL, teens, good-looking.
RACHEL, Nick's mother, comely, 40s.
HAL, Paul's father, 40s, trendy.
CLELA, 20s, American, a model.
ERNEST, thin, 50s.
SCOTTIE, heavily built, late 30s.
ANN, teens, middle-class accent.
JOY, 40ish, full-bodied, black hair, white face, intense.
RAYMOND, Nick's father, 50s, well-built.

THE SOCIALISTS

ACT ONE

ACT ONE SCENE ONE

A Committee Room in the House of Commons. Time – the present.

> **ANN**
> *(Offstage.)*
> No, no, quite all right. I'm early ... Not at all ... thank you, I'm fine.

ANN enters – an attractive woman in her forties. She wears functional but elegant clothes and has a good hair-cut. She looks at the papers laid out for the meeting, peruses them with close attention. Then she turns at a sound.

PAUL enters. He is in his forties, less formally dressed, lean, tanned, good-looking, with an intelligent face.

> **ANN**
> *(Smiling politely)*
> Another early arrival.

> **PAUL**
> Hullo. Congratulations on the appointment.

> **ANN**
> Culture, Media and Sport. Not known as preferment.
> She smiles at him in enquiry.

> **ANN**
> Don't I know you?

THE SOCIALISTS

She peers into his face, then jerks back in surprise and recognition.

                ANN

Paul!

                PAUL

Ann!

They stare at each other and then embrace warmly. PAUL steps back, shaking his head in wonder.

                PAUL
I didn't ... I had no idea you were Ann Phillipson – *the* Ann.

                ANN
Different surname. Married name.

                PAUL
You didn't keep your own name, Ann Vernon?

                ANN
No. Well, you know – the kids.

                PAUL

Kids?

                ANN
Two boys and a girl. You?

                PAUL
I have a son. He lives with his mother in Wisconsin.

                ANN
Do you see him?

                PAUL
Oh yes. So, are we going to get anything?

ACT ONE

ANN

Not a lot. As little as possible, but something. You're here for –?

PAUL

Trees.

ANN

Oh Paul! Of course. It was always trees.

PAUL

(Surprised.)

Was it?

ANN

Oh yes! We were in Hyde Park once, and you said that town parks made you claustrophobic but that the trees were superbly tended. Model forestry. *(Slight pause.)* I read your book on the Amazon. Where are you living – what country?

PAUL

Oh, here and there. I move about. You've moved about a bit yourself.

ANN

Well, keep on trucking as we used to say. *(She smiles at him.)* Funny though – us both being here.

PAUL

Yeah.

ANN

Plus ça change, eh? It's very good to see you.

PAUL

You too.

ANN

I feel quite fortified!

PAUL shakes his head, quizzically.

PAUL

Uh ... as the Minister, you're the enemy.

ANN

Well, as I say – plus ça change! *(They laugh.)* How is your mother?

PAUL

Moira? Fine – "Look, we have come through!" She married a New Zealander with a farm the size of Devon. My father's still sulking after calling her a loser and doing her out of the house.

ANN

I liked Moira.

Light change.

A large sign is illuminated saying: 'The Early Seventies.'

ACT ONE SCENE TWO

A Fashion Store Changing Room. The Early Seventies.

MOIRA, stands in front of a store mirror (as ANN and PAUL exit unobtrusively.) MOIRA has tried on a droopy long dress in swirly purple and brown. The medieval sleeves are too tight and the dress displays her stomach. The SHOP ASSISTANT looms up behind her.

SHOP ASSISTANT

How are you getting on? Ooh that looks nice!

ACT ONE

She catches MOIRA'S eye.

SHOP ASSISTANT
I'll see what else I can find. *(Goes.)*

MOIRA
No, don't go ...

She struggles out of the dress, sinks onto a spindly chair, looks at herself in her discoloured underwear. The SHOP ASSISTANT erupts again through the curtains.

SHOP ASSISTANT
What about a trouser suit?

MOIRA just looks at her.

There is a moment of truth between them.

MOIRA
Thanks anyway.

SHOP ASSISTANT
Sorry.

She disappears. MOIRA looks at herself in the glass, rises, grabs her stuff and wanders off in her underwear.

Light change.

ACT ONE SCENE THREE

Three YOUTHS erupt onstage. These are NICK, PAUL and TOBY. They all wear school blazers. They play around robustly, shouting hoarsely. CLAIRE, an attractive teenage girl, walks past. TOBY, a dark boy with a pudding hair-cut and a somewhat Asiatic face, throws himself at her feet, and propels himself on his back in front of her. She sidesteps him deftly, and he jumps up.

> TOBY
>
> *(Calls after her.)*
>
> Hey Claire, your arse wobbles!

She turns and clouts him with her schoolbag. It is a well-aimed blow and he staggers. NICK, a dark, pudgy boy, takes CLAIRE suavely by the arm.

> NICK
>
> *(US accent.)*
>
> Hey, baby, I hadda come.

> CLAIRE
>
> Get off!

The boys box her in.

> NICK
>
> *(US accent.)*
>
> If you'd only let me Explain!

She dodges them, giving PAUL, the third boy – who is good-looking – a challenging stare. He turns away.

> CLAIRE
>
> Anyway, why weren't you lot at the meeting?

> PAUL
>
> De Forrest was there.

> NICK
>
> Yeah, real coup. Big asset. That guy's going to be England's first black Harold Wilson.

> TOBY
>
> No, he's not.

ACT ONE

PAUL

He's got a trial for West Ham.

NICK

You're kidding! A schwarzer?

CLAIRE

(Dismissive)

Football! *(To PAUL.)* You'd better make the next one. Joy was very pissed off.

She slings her bag on her shoulder, gives PAUL another challenging stare and goes.

PAUL

(To TOBY.)

Was she pissed off?

TOBY

(Shrugs)

We're not speaking. I said I'd do the leaflets.

NICK jerks his head at PAUL.

NICK

That was *his* fault.

PAUL

I forgot.

NICK

You always forget.

PAUL

What about you, bourgeois hyena?

NICK

I couldn't miss it, it was a Cagney film!

THE SOCIALISTS

PAUL

(To TOBY.)

When's the next one?

TOBY

Tomorrow.

PAUL

God, I hate meetings. My stomach goes like the fucking clappers. Are meetings a mammalian anomaly or is there something wrong with me?

TOBY

You just need to get your end away, mate.

He gives them a rictus smile and lopes off. off. They look at him, and watch him go out of hearing range.

PAUL

I reckon he's going funny in the head.

NICK

What makes you think that?

PAUL

Him and his mother.

NICK

Yeah, weird. *(Going.)* Ciao.

PAUL

(Calls after him.)

Hey, did you do the essay on Pitt?

NICK

(Walking backwards.)

Yeah ...

ACT ONE

PAUL
And you've bloody given it in!

NICK
(Going, calls.)
Had to do something to bring her on.

He exits.

PAUL grins, then moves about, moody and indecisive. Finding no solution to his problems, he exits.

Light change.

ACT ONE SCENE FOUR

NICK, at home, lies sprawled on his bed, listening to BOB DYLAN, joining in with his guitar and ad-libbing vocals. RACHEL, his mother, a comely woman, successfully dressed in warm colours (she likes velvet), enters, laden with expensive shopping bags.

NICK
Been shopping?

RACHEL
Sweaters!

She hauls them out of the shiny bags.

NICK
Six? What you want to buy six for?

RACHEL
Because we can afford it. *(She smooths a sweater.)* Cashmere – beautiful. Don't wear it when you're eating, Nicky, or I'll kill you.

THE SOCIALISTS

NICK

Ma!

RACHEL

And don't look Protestant at me. Buy and sell– buy and sell. You have to turn money round eight times a year otherwise the world stops spinning.

NICK

Come again?

RACHEL

It's what I read. And if you'd gone away to a good school like we wanted ... Never mind. There's no shame in being well-dressed, what's wrong with looking good? You're a beautiful boy – find some new friends. Nice ones and –oh, by the way – Ruthie and her mother are coming for dinner tomorrow. Don't forget. She's a lovely girl.

NICK

I'm not old enough to get married.

RACHEL

(Laughs.)

Get married ... get married! *(She hugs him fondly and kisses him. He doesn't mind this.)* Such a handsome boy!

She goes.

NICK strums his guitar, then drops it, and puts on a sweater.

NICK

(Muttering to himself.)

Buy and sell ... buy and sell ... buy and sell ...

ACT ONE

He puts on a loud golfing cap and exits.

Light change.

ACT ONE SCENE FIVE

PAUL and MOIRA at home.

He wears an old raincoat nearly down to his feet, tied with string, and an Aussie hat, turned up at one side. It is too big, low on the brow, making him look mental. MOIRA gazes at him without expression.

PAUL
Don't look like that, I have to see him, he's my father, anyway I'm broke.

MOIRA
I hate it.

PAUL
Why? It's finished, done with. You're not jealous of her, are you?

MOIRA
She's young.

PAUL
Production line, this week's offer! They're not in your class – either of them. *(She sniffs.)* Mum, for Christ's sake! All right, I won't go.

MOIRA
No, go. Go. I can't ... it's ...

PAUL
Get another man. Why not?

MOIRA tries to recover.

>MOIRA
>
>*(Hopeless smile.)*
>
>The Avon lady made up my face. What do you think?

>PAUL
>
>No, it looks silly. You don't need ... It's not your style. You could lose some weight.

>MOIRA
>
>*(Furious.)*
>
>Oh, get out!

Light change.

ACT ONE SCENE SIX

PAUL at his father's flat in Holland Park.

His father, HAL, is trendy, careful, and tough. His girlfriend CLELA, is an American model in her mid-twenties.

>HAL
>
>Well, if not university, then what?

CLELA pushes a big bowl of dip towards PAUL, and a dish of crackers. He sticks his finger in the dip and licks it.

>PAUL
>
>Dunno. Bum around, I guess. I could try a bit of business.

>HAL
>
>Don't even think about it.

ACT ONE

PAUL

The money's good. Okay. Okay, how about a handout?

HAL

Not a good moment I'm afraid.

PAUL

When is it going to be a good moment?

HAL

I paid for your trip to Iceland – and your teeth.

PAUL sticks his fingers in the dip, swirls them round and round.

HAL

Don't do that!

PAUL looks in mock-innocent enquiry.

HAL

It's offensive.

PAUL

Why? My hands are clean.

CLELA

(American accent.)

It is offensive because you do it to offend.

PAUL

Could be. *(He licks his fingers.)* Ugh!

CLELA

What?

PAUL

Why mash the fruits of the earth into smooth sick?

CLELA

(Baffled.)

It's supposed to be like that.

THE SOCIALISTS

His father hands him a fiver.

                HAL

Here. Buzz off.

PAUL makes no move to take the money.

                HAL

Suit yourself.

He pockets the fiver, and turns away.

                PAUL

I don't blame you, I'm surprised you stayed so long.

                HAL

Shut up.

                PAUL

It's just ...

PAUL, suddenly weary, puts on the ludicrous golf cap.

                HAL

It's not as simple as you ...

                PAUL

I know.

                HAL

Not diagnosable at the drop of a hat.

                PAUL

I've said, I know! *(He picks up his bag.)* I'm getting the weight of her depressions now.

                HAL

Oh God.

PAUL starts to go.

ACT ONE

HAL

Look, I've been thinking ...

PAUL

(Turns, murderous.)

Don't. *(Slight pause as he recovers himself.)* You're a disappointment.

HAL gestures, mystified.

PAUL

Matter of taste. She has it, you don't. *(He wheels, waving an arm at the decor.)* What the fuck did all this cost! How many years was it? Solicitor's secretary, export supervisor, dogsbody for hauliers, repping, while you sat at home "freelancing", and ringing your bloody girlfriends!

HAL shoots a look at CLELA, who looks back levelly.

PAUL

She cooked your meals, washed your clothes, made you read, had the ideas, wrote your promos, your job applications – mocked up interviews for you, bam, bam, bam ... bingo! Soft-top Merc, expensive deodorant, platinum credit card ...

HAL

And I'm grateful for ...

PAUL

There was still no money for the bloody gas bill. No Shangri-La on the domestic front.

HAL

That's enough! Moira has her own style. She makes her own choices – she always has.

THE SOCIALISTS

CLELA

And I'd love to help! If she would just – relate a little. I know Moira thinks ... But I do have insights into her problems. I'm a woman. We have things in common ...

PAUL, as he goes, gives her such a threatening look that she prudently steps out of the way. HAL, his father, rises angrily but PAUL is quick, and backs away.

HAL

(Containing himself.)

Give my regards to your mother. If she has any more trouble with the car, tell her to let me know. I'll see if I can fix a trade in.

PAUL

The old banger? We sold that last winter to pay the plumber.

He exits.

Silence. HAL sits, and makes a show of relaxing. He looks across to CLELA.

HAL

Show me something nice.

Slowly, she takes out one tit.

Light change.

ACT ONE SCENE SEVEN

Living Room in the house of Toby's mother, JOY.

A large poster with a badly-drawn clenched fist. A rickety table, odd chairs, dirty cups, saucers full of cigarette ends. TOBY is at

ACT ONE

the table doing his French homework with the aid of a dictionary. ERNEST enters – a spare-framed man in his early fifties, in an old navy coat, shiny with age. He enters as if by habit, takes off his coat, folds it and puts it to one side.

ERNEST

Where's your Mum? *(TOBY goes on with his work.)* It's nearly half-past!

He collects the teacups, puts them on a piece of board that acts as a tray, and exits. SCOTTIE enters – a big man who looks older than his thirty-seven years. He and TOBY acknowledge each other with nods. TOBY looks up translations in his dictionary.

TOBY

She's not back yet.

SCOTTIE nods, sits, and looks at the racing results in his evening paper. Pause. NICK and PAUL enter.

NICK

Hi, Scottie.

PAUL

'Lo, Scott.

SCOTTIE

(Glasgow accent.)

Hullo to ye.

NICK offers SCOTTIE his cigarettes. He takes one.

SCOTTIE

Thanks. *(He lights up with an enormous lighter.)*

PAUL and NICK lurch onto TOBY, cribbing over his shoulder.

THE SOCIALISTS

PAUL

Hey is that the French homework?

TOBY

(Not stopping them.)

Get off.

CLAIRE enters. They nod at her casually.

CLAIRE

Well?

NICK

What?

CLAIRE

Have you brought them? The leaflets!

PAUL

Oh Christ, I forgot.

SCOTTIE

Won't get the revolution that way.

NICK

Where's Joy?

TOBY

Out.

ERNEST enters with a large enamel pot of tea, cups, sugar, and a bottle of milk. They all fall on it – NICK grabbing the large mug.

CLAIRE

Hey, that's Scottie's!

She wrests the mug from NICK, pours tea, adds milk, gives it to SCOTTIE, who is very chuffed by her attention.

SCOTTIE

Thanks, hen.

ACT ONE

ANN enters.

She is dressed down, but her jeans are over-neat. Her manner is bright, breezy and manic.

ANN
(Middle-class accent.)

Hi everybody. Am I late?

ERNEST

Joy's not here yet.

ANN

I was on the demo. Honestly, the fucking fuzz! I was lucky not to get my head bashed in!

SCOTTIE
(Soberly.)

They had the whangers out, eh?

ANN

I thought they were going to, any minute.

PAUL turns away from her dismissively.

ANN
(Agitated at the snub.)

There was a terrific turnout!

NICK

What was it for?

ANN
(Showing him up for not knowing.)

The Bolivians!

Honour restored, she smiles around.

ANN

Oh good, tea!

They settle down around the table. ERNEST, on his feet, pours.

The chair at the head of the table is kept vacant. SCOTTIE sits to the left of it. ERNEST, wants to sit on the right, but is beaten to it by PAUL. He's about to protest, and bangs down the teapot, leaving them to help themselves. Then sits at the other end. NICK is left without a seat.

TOBY sees this, rises, gives NICK his seat, and exits. He re-enters immediately with an old plastic Sanibin, empties the rubbish in one chuck into the corner, upends the bin and sits on it. They drink tea.

NICK

Any biscuits?

Thwarted, he bends to his tea.

SCOTTIE
(To TOBY.)
Did she say she'd be late?

TOBY shrugs. ERNEST rises, crosses, gets a sheaf of papers from his coat pocket and hands them round.

ERNEST

Minutes from the last meeting.

They all look these over.

CLAIRE

What does it mean, Point 2.D? "Recommended that the group proceed with the setting up of a procedural mechanism to be ratified by future working party stroke meetings."

ANN

Oh, it's quite simple. You weren't here. It just means that each meeting constitutes a meeting of the working party.

ACT ONE

CLAIRE

I can see that. I'm querying the meaning of group, meeting and working party. There are at least two opposing definitions here.

ANN

It's quite simple.

CLAIRE

No, it's not. It bloody isn't! Who wrote up the minutes?

PAUL

Ern.

ERNEST

It was decided to leave the definitions of all terms open after a general discussion.

TOBY

After a fucking row.

ANN

Nonsense, there wasn't a row, it was ...

NICK

A heated discussion, leading to a stand-off ...

PAUL

A bloody row.

CLAIRE

(Looking at the paper.)
This is going to need a lot of clarification.

ANN

(Hot.)
There's nothing to clarify! All the terms were defined. *(To PAUL)* Right?

PAUL looks up at her mildly, irritating her.

ANN

Scottie? Ernest? Ernest? *(Gesturing for him to speak.)*

ERNEST

I propose we wait for Joy.

SCOTTIE

Seconded.

NICK

(Murmurs.)

Speak of the devil.

JOY enters. She is a full-bosomed woman with black hair and a face that's intense, passionate, and almost indecently alive. Her eyes bulge frighteningly when she is worked up. She is ferocious. A really frightening woman. She looks round. NICK smiles at her ingratiatingly.

JOY

(To NICK.)

What are you grinning at?

Silence. ERNEST wipes out a mug, pours JOY tea, and adds three spoonfuls of sugar.

SCOTTIE

(To JOY.)

Declare the meeting open?

JOY nods.

SCOTTIE

Who's going to chair?

Silence.

ACT ONE

SCOTTIE

Propose Joy to take the chair.

NICK

(Prompt.)

Seconded.

SCOTTIE

Joy?

She nods. ERNEST walks the length of the table, deposits papers before her.

ERNEST

Minutes. *(She looks up at him evilly.)* Oh, you've got a copy of course. Sorry about that. *(Pompous and loud.)* So, who's going to read the minutes? Toby?

TOBY, head down, picks his teeth. ERNEST looks at PAUL and NICK, dismisses them, then looks at ANN, who half-rises. ERNEST makes to reject her but CLAIRE, seeing this, rises.

CLAIRE

I'll do it.

ANN, puzzled, sits back.

ANN

D'you think you should? You weren't here last week.

NICK

Okay, I'll read them if that's all right. *(He reads quickly before any argument.)* "Jim McBride went through the minutes of the previous meeting. Ann Morris and Jim agreed … "

ERNEST

(Correcting him.)

Jim McBride …

THE SOCIALISTS

NICK

Jim McBride agreed that Ernest Thompson's request to constitute the group was, in fact, a "formalisation..." *(To JOY, who scrapes her chair loudly.)* What?

JOY

This is no bloody good.

SCOTTIE

What's wrong wi' it?

JOY

Bloody *names* all over everything! Burn the lot.

CLAIRE
(As ERNEST makes to pick up all the papers.)

We can't use our own names?

JOY

What do you think?!

ERNEST

Joy's right.

PAUL

Good, can we have code names?

NICK

Great! What you going to call yourself, Tobe?

TOBY

Sausage.

PAUL
(To NICK.)

Nick? Cheese Roll? Egg on Toast?

ACT ONE

NICK

Sabra.

CLAIRE

Sabra? What's that?

NICK

Well, in Israel it means a native Israeli-born citizen. The original meaning is the fruit of the prickly pear. Tough on the outside, sweet as honey inside.

ANN

(Charmed.)

Oh, Nick!

CLAIRE

(Cheerfully.)

Sounds like a girl's name – *(to ANN.)* What about you? Princess Anne? Lady Penelope?

ANN

Haven't a clue.

NICK

Ernie, you could be Fred, for Fred Engels.

ERNEST

Are you trying to be funny?

He rises, angry. JOY cuts across. She points round the table in turn.

JOY

A, B, C, D, E, F, G, H. Okay?

NICK

What am I? I've forgotten what I am.

They all count and say, severally, "F."

TOBY

You're F.

NICK

So I am.

ERNEST

Well get on then!

NICK

What? Oh, I'm reading the minutes, yeah? Hang on. *(Mutters under his breath, getting to his place.)* Right then. *(Takes a deep breath, then ...)* Do you want me to put in the code names as I go along, Joy?

ANN

We might as well get into the habit.

SCOTTIE

Ye'll slow things up.

PAUL

No, go on. We'll sort it out later.

NICK

(Reads.)

"Point two. Ernest Thompson was asked to read the resolutions drafted by the previous meeting. He reported that these resolutions coincided with the procedural points which he had also been requested to formulate, fourteen in all. He then proceeded to read the resolutions and then the fourteen proposals. Jim McBride at this point asked if there were any objections from those present to deciding on a procedural mechanism. There were no objections."

CLAIRE

Point of order – there were.

ACT ONE

JOY

Later.

CLAIRE

There were objections, Joy. You yourself...

JOY

I said later.

NICK

Shall I go on?

TOBY

(Mutters.)

Oh God.

NICK

I'll go on. *(Reads:)* "The present working party stroke meeting recommended that the group proceed with the setting up of a procedural mechanism to be ratified by future working parties stroke meetings. Point three. Ernest's recommendations, see Point two, were discussed and a start was made for them to be set out as recommended for future working parties stroke meetings."

CLAIRE sighs impatiently.

ANN

You'll see exactly what we mean in the next point!

NICK

"Point three..."

ERNEST

Point four.

CLAIRE

Point four.

THE SOCIALISTS

NICK

Sorry. "Point four. It was suggested and agreed that, semi-colon, Working Party will in future mean all those in the group listed in Number One of Ernest's recommendations, working towards setting up a constitution for the group. And that Meeting will refer to those members of the working party present at one particular meeting."

CLAIRE

What's happened to "the Group?"

PAUL

Gone up in fag smoke. Anybody got a cigarette?

NICK

Help yourself. "The meeting then formally adjourned as Jim McBride was drunk and Joy and Ernest had to leave for the Hoxton protest. There was an hour of self-criticism and it was suggested that this week's meeting should include formal inter-criticism as a follow-on."

ANN

We might as well get in the habit.

SCOTTIE

Nah-nah. No more wanks.

ANN

Why not?

SCOTTIE

Okay, hen.

ANN

Hang on, we haven't had the meeting yet. We've only heard the minutes!

ACT ONE

ERNEST

(To JOY.)

Break for a cuppa, Joy? *(Aside.)* I've got a drop of something.

JOY

Suit yourselves.

NICK

Whose turn is it to make tea? Draw straws?

No-one responds.

NICK

Oh, all right.

He exits, followed by ANN with the cups and pot, which he has forgotten. JOY and ERNIE confer.

ANN

(Entering.)

Shall we start the criticism? We might as well. I'm dying for my turn.

CLAIRE

What?

ANN

I do think I was as self-critical as anybody last week.

CLAIRE

(Aloud, to PAUL.)

Did the poor little rich girl bite the dust again?

ANN

Being working class doesn't necessarily confer All the virtues, Claire. I have done as much for this group as you – in fact a bloody sight more.

CLAIRE
Well you've got the time, haven't you?

ANN
Yes, I have, and this is what I choose to do with it. I could be sitting on the beach in St Tropez, I don't see why I should be penalized quite so much.

SCOTTIE
No, you're fine. *(He moves close. ANN moves away prudently.)*

PAUL
Oh, by the way, I can't be here next week. I'm doing an interview.

SCOTTIE
Where?

PAUL
Cambridge. Don't worry, I'm passing on it – even if I get in, which is very unlikely.

ANN
Yes, and I shall be away from the ... *(looks at her large leather-covered diary)* ... from the tenth to the nineteenth.

TOBY
Where you going?

ANN
To see my people.

CLAIRE
The villa?

ANN
The villa, Claire. With the four bathrooms, all en suite.

ACT ONE

CLAIRE

Hitching, are you?

ANN

No, I'm going by plane. Want to come?

CLAIRE

Sorry, I'm going shark fishing.

PAUL

Shut up, both of you.

CLAIRE

Sexist!

ANN

Chauvinist!

A loud crash, and sounds of breaking china, offstage.

NICK enters.

NICK

Sorry. Sorry, Joy. I'll pay for it ...

CLAIRE

Oh Christ.

NICK

Got any glasses?

SCOTTIE

Sit down, for Chrissakes.

NICK

Sorry.

JOY seems un-phased.

PAUL

Okay. So ... who's going to start the criticism? Who loves me most?

CLAIRE

Frivolous bastard.

NICK

Now, now ... We haven't all had your privileged background, oh orthodox commie princess.

ANN

Let's go round the table. Scottie?

SCOTTIE

Fook that. *(To PAUL:)* You're so bloody keen, you start. Kick off with Claire.

He knows PAUL fancies CLAIRE.

CLAIRE

Me?

PAUL

Why not? Okay. Ready? Claire. Full of shit ... Bloody know-all ... Sharp as a needle ... good attendance in the group. Could be making bread modelling ... Works in Boots on Saturday to help her Mum.

NICK

Can I be best man?

PAUL

Shut up. Full of crappy ideology. Looks like she's going to kill you if you say the words America or Trotsky ...

CLAIRE

What's that supposed to mean?

ACT ONE

PAUL

That your childhood was insular and prejudiced.

CLAIRE

Thank you.

NICK

Her father will be round to beat you up in the morning.

PAUL

She's the best revolutionary we have.

Chorus of "oohs" from TOBY and NICK. CLAIRE is out of face.

PAUL

But bossy.

CLAIRE

Fuck off.

PAUL

Right, Rosa Luxemburg. Now, let me see ...

He looks around the group. NICK cringes, ANN looks eager, ERNEST glares.

PAUL

Ernest. *(ERNEST eyeballs him threateningly.)*
Marxist-Leninist theorist. *(Pause.)* Or so he believes.

ERNEST

What?

PAUL

Ernest is a religious man ...

SCOTTIE
(Baffled.)

Religious?

PAUL

... his thinking shaped and confined by chapel-going stroke trade unionist background ...

A chorus of disagreement. ERNEST looks ready for a punch-up.

PAUL

Order! Order! Just teasing.

SCOTTIE

What is it, Ernie?

ERNEST

Later.

ANN

Go on, Paul.

PAUL looks around the table. TOBY, head down, is doodling furiously.

PAUL

Toby.

TOBY looks up, surprised.

PAUL

Toby. Son and heir of the founder of our group. Plays with his cards glued to his nipples. Genuine Marxist? Hard to say. Committed Revolutionary? Or is he just keeping Mum happy?

TOBY looks up with a steely glance.

PAUL

Why so secretive, brother?

It is a personal appeal, that hangs in the air.

ACT ONE

ANN

Is that all? *(To TOBY)* You didn't get much of a going over.

PAUL

Ann.

ANN

Yes.

PAUL

Disaffected.

ANN

Is that all?

PAUL

That's all.

ANN
(Disappointed.)

What?

SCOTTIE

Can ye no expand a wee bit, Paul? The girl needs feedback.

PAUL

What do you want me to say? Brought up by servants, sent away to school at six.

ANN

What has that got ...

PAUL

The night I walked you home and met your mother ...

ANN

What?

THE SOCIALISTS

PAUL

You knifed her. Bam, bam, bam! It was vicious.

ANN

What's that got to ...

PAUL

Chronic case of disaffection. Name it, she'll protest about it. Politically illiterate, mentally lazy, quarrelsome, inadequate, and dangerous.

ANN

Oh, now look here. Is this supposed to be a character assassination session? That's a load of rubbish. Really, it's so immature. There's no room for this sort of petty spite. I mean, I'm prepared to take criticism. It was Joy who said we leave our personal lives outside when we come through the door ...

PAUL

(Cutting her off.)

Nevertheless, she has one immensely valuable asset to this group. Energy. Her energy. She's loaded with it. And it's on offer. To us. She doesn't need to be here. We're not in her interest. Technically she's our enemy. An enemy of the people – a target for destruction. But here she is. Doing most of the paperwork and – when she doesn't try to talk politics – she's terrific.

ANN

Thank you.

PAUL

Not at all. Scottie.

ACT ONE

SCOTTIE

Right, man.

PAUL

Works hard. Drinks too much. Thinks he's God's gift to women when he's drunk. *(Laughter)* Has no will to power. Makes other people's will to power seem unworthy ... You're a lovely man, Scott. You make us better than we are. And if Scotland is so bloody great, why did you come down here?

Laughter. PAUL looks round the table. ERNEST and JOY are conferring again. JOY looks up at the sudden quiet.

SCOTTIE

Joy. Paul's ready to take you on.

JOY

Break over. Agenda. Proposals for working party procedure – then Finance. Then, Action. *(On the last word she leans forward, eyes bulging mesmerically.)*

ANN

Good!

JOY

I'll read the proposals for the working party procedure.

CLAIRE

To be ratified.

JOY glares at her.

SCOTTIE
(To JOY)

Open discussion?

JOY

(Grimaces, then reads.)

"One. Until a constitution and principles are agreed upon, each meeting of what was called The Group is considered a working party to set up a constitution that is a definition of the group. Two. Each meeting passes on its work as a responsibility to the next working party. Three. Meetings of the working party will be weekly, with frequent changes of venue, day and time. Four. Each meeting will have a chair, by rota, and be minuted. Five. A quorum will be five. Six. Agendas for meetings will be drawn up by the previous working party. It is the responsibility of all members to keep in contact if they miss a meeting. Seven. If new matters are to be dealt with, they should be added to the agenda after the previous week's minutes have been read."

PAUL and NICK show signs of restlessness.

JOY

Eight. A working party which is a quorum, and has reached agreement on an issue, is empowered by the whole membership to propose it for voting. Nine. The working party must decide whether issues are constitutional and therefore require voting on by the total membership, or expedient, in which case the working party can ratify, to be finally approved by the membership.

CLAIRE

So, everything will be ratified by the total membership?

She and JOY lock stares.

ACT ONE

CLAIRE

It's important.

JOY

"Ten. For all voting within working parties, or full membership, a two-thirds majority is required.' *(To CLAIRE:)* Satisfied?

CLAIRE

Not entirely, no.

JOY

"Eleven. Each member has one vote. Twelve. All members are members until decided otherwise by the group. Individualistic resignation will not be allowed. There are no excuses for failure to attend meetings or to be unaware of time or venue. All members must be up to date with group work. Lateness will not be tolerated."

SCOTTIE

Does this not assume that all meetings will be fully attended? Is the term working party therefore not now rendered obsolete?

Some groans.

ANN

Scottie, we thrashed all this out last week.

CLAIRE

What a load of shit. Of course, we can't all be here for every meeting. Are you nuts? Scottie's on construction. He doesn't know where he'll be week to week! All this crap about meetings and working parties – now we've all got to be here, on the dot, every bloody ... Some of us have to earn a living! I'm in the school play – apart from working nights at Sandy's.

ERNEST
It's a declaration of intent.

CLAIRE
Are you crackers? You can't declare your intention to do the impossible.

ANN
We've been thrashing this out for six months. Some of us want action.

The BOYS are making covert signals of agreement to leave.

JOY hands papers to ERNEST to be handed round.

JOY
Procedural suggestions. Read them. Any amendments to be tabled for discussion next week. Who's taking the minutes? Isn't anybody taking the minutes?

ANN
I've been making notes.

JOY
Ratification to take place next week and amendments to be discussed and voted. Item two on the agenda... Finance.

Groans at the word 'finance.' SCOTTIE tips the ash out of the big ash-tray, blows the rest in everyone's face and sends it round for contributions. PAUL pokes about uselessly in his pockets. TOBY makes for the door.

JOY
Where are you going?

TOBY
Violin practice.

ACT ONE

PAUL and NICK rise.

NICK

We've gotta go.

JOY

Where?

SCOTTIE

Aye and what's happened to your friend, the wee black feller?

NICK

De Forrest? That's where we're going to find out, right Paul?

PAUL

We think he may have gone over to the SWP.

ERNEST

Bloody right-wing fascists. Trust them to hoover up the spades.

CLAIRE shakes her head and laughs at this.

NICK

We're nipping over to infiltrate.

PAUL

Yeah. Do a recce.

Some suspicion of the truth of this. ERNEST consults JOY. She looks brutal.

ERNEST

(Mutters to JOY.)

His name may have to go on the list.

PAUL

List? What list? *(Silence.)* I'm sorry but – what list?

TOBY

(At the door.)

Are you coming?

PAUL

What are you going to do to him?

JOY

Wouldn't you like to know!

CLAIRE

What's all this about?

PAUL

Yes, I would. I would like to know. I'm a fully paid up member of this group, well, a member of this group. I don't know of any list. *(To ANN)* Do you know anything about it? *(To CLAIRE)* Do you? Look, De Forrest's kosher. He's not some fucking elite, pseudo-fascist dick-wagging shit-face ... What list?

Silence. JOY sneers.

PAUL

Right. I submit an item for next week's agenda. Discussion of secret list mentioned at this meeting by him *(Points at ERNEST.)* Full and open discussion. Vote to be taken.

JOY

Are you going, or staying?

PAUL

Going?

JOY

Well piss off then.

The BOYS go. Silence.

ACT ONE

ERNEST

Bloody little entrepreneurs. They think we're a good laugh.

JOY

Because that is what we are.

ERNEST

I'm not joking. This isn't funny.

JOY

Yes, it is. We all are.

ANN

Joy's right. They're just making fun of us.

ERNEST

So, I'm a joke, am I?

SCOTTIE

Aye well, the new élite ... Comprehensives.

ANN

They're so immature!

CLAIRE

Yeah, like you – going on about the noble proletariat.

JOY

(To CLAIRE, silky.)

Ready for action, are you?

CLAIRE

You know where I stand, Joy.

JOY

Oh, we know that.

CLAIRE

I don't believe in it.

JOY

(Mocking her.)

"I don't believe in it!"

ANN

Believe in what?

SCOTTIE

Direct action.

CLAIRE rises, puts on her jacket.

CLAIRE

Violence. *(She approaches JOY, leans down, nose to nose.)* Not one hair of one baby's head.

ANN

Oh, honestly, that is so romantic.

ERNEST and JOY look at her with interest and exchange a glance.

ERNEST

Pub? Drink?

JOY

I'm closing the meeting. *(To ANN.)* You can do the minutes.

ANN

Right, Joy. Look! *(The BOYS have left their sheets.)* Typical!

CLAIRE

Some of those are Toby's. He lives here.

ERNEST

(To JOY.)

A couple of drinks round the corner?

ACT ONE

JOY

(Shakes her head.)

I need to talk to Scottie.

JOY and SCOTTIE leave. ERNEST is very put out. ANN tidies officiously, grabs her bag, waves and goes.

CLAIRE

You want to get tough with Joy, Ernie.

ERNEST

Why don't you mind your own business?

CLAIRE

It's what she respects.

ERNEST

And you'd know?

CLAIRE

Yes, I would.

ERNEST

Shut your mouth.

CLAIRE

Sorry I spoke.

ERNEST

Let me tell you something. When the revolution comes, you'll be first on my list.

She backs off, horrified by his venom, and goes. He grabs his coat, stands, controlling his fury – and leaves.

Fade to black.

END OF ACT ONE.

ACT TWO

ACT TWO SCENE ONE

A London Coffee Bar.

JIMI HENDRIX is playing on the sound system. PAUL, NICK and TOBY are at a table, drinking coffee.

>> PAUL

No!

>> TOBY

Oh yes.

NICK leans back, listening to the music.

>> PAUL

Guns? They've got guns?

>> TOBY

Yeah.

>> PAUL

What sort of guns?

>> TOBY

They've got a shotgun, a rifle. At least one pistol. Maybe two.

>> PAUL

With ammunition?

>> TOBY

Yeah – and bombs.

>> PAUL

Bombs?

ACT TWO

TOBY

Small ones. Well, the stuff to make them with.

NICK
(Raising his voice above the music)
What are they going to do with them? With the guns?

He looks round to make sure they are not overheard.

TOBY

Use them.

PAUL

On what?

TOBY

People.

PAUL

Who? Anyone in particular, or just people in general?

TOBY

I don't know. The Lord Mayor? Ted Heath?

PAUL

What for?

NICK

Because they're there.

TOBY

Yeah.

PAUL

You really mean they're going to blow people up?

TOBY

Yeah.

PAUL

You mean, Lords – famous people – MPs?

TOBY

Well, not necessarily. Not if it means a long bus ride. It could be that Tory bastard on Kensington Council.

PAUL

Anybody right-wing.

TOBY

Or Labour. Tony Benn's no safer than Enoch.

NICK

Tread softly, Michael Foot.

PAUL rises, paces briefly, and then sits.

PAUL

Toby, you don't really mean they're gonna kill somebody?

TOBY

Yeah, I think they might. I think they could.

PAUL

Your Mum?

TOBY looks at him without expression.

PAUL

Scottie? – Nah. Ernest? But what for?

TOBY

They think society's rotten.

PAUL

But they're society. We're society. We're all rotten. Why don't they kill themselves?

NICK

I doubt that's the idea. *(Points two fingers at his temple.)* Boom-boom. Nah.

ACT TWO

PAUL

But your Mum's had kids, for God's sake!

TOBY

So?

PAUL

Well, I don't know. I mean, I don't think Moira could do us in. She's put so much time into, you know, keeping us going. I mean, I know she's a pain in the neck. *(To TOBY.)* Where do they keep them? The guns?

TOBY

Dunno.

PAUL

Can you find out?

TOBY

They're a bit suspicious.

PAUL

It's her. Your fucking mother. You ought to do something.

NICK

What about Ann? Is she in on it?

TOBY

(Screws his face, wags his head. He's not sure.)

Could be. She knows where they stash it, or she did. She used to clean them.

PAUL

Used to? Not now?

THE SOCIALISTS

TOBY

Dunno.

NICK

(Serious)

Give her a fuck, she'll tell you.

TOBY pulls a face of disgust. NICK turns to PAUL.

NICK

All right, you then.

ANN enters.

PAUL

What about you? You can pull her now. She's just come in the door.

NICK

(His back to ANN.)

Oh, very funny.

ANN looms up beside him, and he falls off his chair. PAUL and TOBY rise quickly.

TOBY

See you, Nick. Hi, Ann.

ANN

What are you lot doing here? You're supposed to be ...

PAUL

Just going ... Cheero!

PAUL and TOBY go. NICK gets back on his chair. ANN sits beside NICK.

ANN

Why aren't you going?

ACT TWO

NICK

I'm Jewish.

ANN

What's that supposed to mean?

NICK

Er ... d'you want a coffee?

ANN

Why, what are you after?

NICK heaves a deep sigh, puts his hand on her crotch. She looks alarmed. He smiles at her gently, earnestly. She begins to soften.

Light change.

ACT TWO SCENE TWO

Nick's parents' bedroom.

Nick's parents – RACHEL and RAYMOND – are dressing to go out to a function. RAYMOND is titivating. RACHEL is ready and looks like a ripe peach. She hands him a folded handkerchief, which he arranges in his breast pocket.

RACHEL

One of the new ones, with your initial.

RAYMOND

Thanks.

He sees to his hair with two brushes, then licks his fingers and smooths his eyebrows. RACHEL has his cologne at the ready. He takes it, and sprays himself.

THE SOCIALISTS

RACHEL

You look fit to eat, Raymond.

RAYMOND

Later darling... Double munchies, eh?

They stand side by side, admiring themselves in the mirror.

RAYMOND

Yup. We're doing well. *(She nods, then looks away.)* What's the matter? What's up?

RACHEL

Nothing.

RAYMOND

What?

RACHEL

It upsets Nicky. Money.

RAYMOND

What?!

RACHEL

He says it's exploitering.

RAYMOND

Exploitering? Exploiting who?

RACHEL

The workers.

RAYMOND

Yeah – you and me. Who works harder than us? Seventy-two on the payroll in London alone, and that's not counting the outworkers.

RACHEL

And you're very fair.

ACT TWO

RAYMOND

Three months off for having a kid. Two weeks for the Dad. What's he on about?

RACHEL

They don't believe in bosses.

RAYMOND

Who?

RACHEL

His group.

RAYMOND

What group?

RACHEL

They're ... I don't know. Alternative. It's political.

RAYMOND

Don't listen to him. He's a kid, Rachel. Politics – what does he know about politics? *We're* politics, pet. We're out there. Buying and selling. Trade. That's what it's all about. The law of contract. A very equitable notion. Take my word. Of course, you get the schmoozers and the con-artists. They're there to keep you awake. Now, are you going to wear the stole?

RACHEL

No-o. The weather's too warm. It'll look like I'm showing off.

He laughs. She joins in. They can't stop laughing.

RACHEL

Oh fuck, I'll wear it.

RAYMOND

Good. And mind the language.

RACHEL

Sorry.

She picks up the mink stole, and strokes it. He puts it reverently around her shoulders and they go.

> *Light change.*

ACT TWO SCENE THREE.

At School.

The SCHOOL BELL rings. PAUL, NICK and CLAIRE enter. A TEACHER pushes past them.

TEACHER

Come on, clear the doorway. *(To PAUL)* Good luck. It's your viva tomorrow, isn't it?

He nods and goes.

PAUL

Piss off. Doesn't even know my name.

CLAIRE

You going?

PAUL pulls a face.

CLAIRE

Well, you better clean yourself up.

TOBY enters. He inspects PAUL severely.

CLAIRE

Look at his zits. Use the Clearasil.

ACT TWO

NICK

Yeah, no good de Forrest lending him the suit if they think he's got the clap.

PAUL groans.

CLAIRE

He's nervous.

PAUL

I am not.

CLAIRE

Go on – admit it.

PAUL

Bollocks. What I ... What I ... What I am waiting for is to meet one human being I don't despise.

CLAIRE

Thanks.

TOBY laughs.

PAUL

Waste of time, tomorrow. If I get it, I'm not going.

CLAIRE

Hah!

CLAIRE hitches her bag and goes.

NICK

Yeah, yeah, yeah.

PAUL

Okay. So, how are you getting on with Mad Ann?

NICK

Perhaps we'll honeymoon in Crete ... or that other one where Aphrodite came out of the foam. But first,

I've got to give Miss Hutchings my essay on Disraeli. See you later.

He goes. Silence.

TOBY

They want to see us.

PAUL

Who?

TOBY

Joy and Ern!

PAUL

What for?

TOBY

Dunno. Something's up. She's ... I don't know.

PAUL

How's Nick getting on with Miss Knightsbridge? Any info?

TOBY

(Shakes his head.)

She won't tell him anything. Coming tonight?

PAUL

I can't. Moira's on a downer.

TOBY

They won't like it.

PAUL

Cover for me. Say I've turned gay. What's she up to, Toby?

TOBY

Dunno.

ACT TWO

PAUL

Why do I think she wants to blow somebody's head off?

TOBY
(Sharp.)

No.

They look at each other. TOBY is hostile. He goes. PAUL watches him go, frowning with worry.

> *Light change.*

ACT TWO SCENE FOUR

In the Kitchen at Moira's.

PAUL and MOIRA. He looks handsome in a dark suit. They sit, side by side, moody.

MOIRA

I blame myself.

Pause.

PAUL

What for?

MOIRA

Encouraging you to be an outsider. It was bloody self-indulgent. Were you rude?

PAUL

No. Actually it was going well. They were pissed as newts. They'd had a good lunch. They even seemed interested in what I was saying.

THE SOCIALISTS

MOIRA

What were you saying?

PAUL

Oh ... I don't know ... stuff about inequality of opportunity – using social workers as sticking plaster. They were all over me. One old girl got quite kittenish.

MOIRA

So why did you walk out?

PAUL

They started to show off. Making snide jokes. Internecine snipes, but not witty enough. Rats in a cage. Not one of them brave enough to put a toe in the water. God, I hate academics.

MOIRA

So, you walked?

PAUL

Yeah. Left them to it.

MOIRA

What did they say?

PAUL

How should I know? Moira, I don't give a fuck. They're a disgrace. They're parasites.

Pause.

MOIRA

We wanted so much for you. After that dreary war – a new start. We voted them in! Parity, decent houses, cheap food, education – a shining civil life for all. Fair

ACT TWO

play. Equal chances. God, what a mess we made of it. They should have gone!

PAUL

Who?

MOIRA

The public schools! Titles. Royalty. We should have made a republic. We could have done it then.

PAUL

You did some good things. You did some good things, Mum. You were green, that's all. Oh, don't cry!

He lifts her, swings her round, and then sets her down.

MOIRA

Pasta?

PAUL

No thanks. Look, d'you mind if I go out?

MOIRA

(He has said the wrong thing)

Of course not. Why should I mind?

PAUL

I'd rather stay in, it's just something I've got to ... It's important.

MOIRA

Trouble?

PAUL

No, no.

MOIRA

You haven't been dealing again?

PAUL

No, I just need to see Toby. Won't be long.

He goes. MOIRA sits, not knowing what to do with herself.

> Light change.

ACT TWO SCENE FIVE.

Nick's bedroom.

NICK is on his bed, strumming his guitar.

RAYMOND
(Offstage.)

Where are you?

RAYMOND enters.

RAYMOND

There you are.

NICK

Yup. What's up?

RAYMOND

Nothing. Your mother's worried, that's all.

NICK

What about?

RAYMOND

She thinks you're in trouble.

NICK

What kind of trouble?

RAYMOND

So long as it isn't drugs. It isn't drugs, is it?

ACT TWO

NICK

No! Well ... cannabis.

RAYMOND

(Shrugs this off.)

She mentioned politics. Is it? Is it politics?

NICK

Yeah. Why not?

RAYMOND

Have you gone mad? Nicky, politics is dangerous. Don't you know that?

NICK

It's the fashion! You know – fashion. What we make a living out of.

RAYMOND

Yeah, flares, anoraks, and Biba and Tommy Nutter rip-offs. Not the same thing. Get out. Now.

NICK

Look, Pop, it's not serious. It's all ... display. One or two head-cases, but they've got nothing going for them. No real power base. It's all fashion. Combat gear, the Red Flag, Ché Guevara, and revolution talk on six hundred quid leather sofas. At least our group is skint.

RAYMOND

You're not making any sense at all.

NICK

Because there is no sense. It's nonsense. I've told you, Dad. it's Fashion.

They look at each other soberly.

Light change.

ACT TWO SCENE SIX

Joy's kitchen.

TOBY and JOY with coffee. A stand-off. She drinks. He drinks.

              JOY

              (Leans over the table.)

Watch out.

              TOBY

Leave it, Mum. Come on!

              JOY

Just watch it.

              TOBY

You think we're going to snitch? Turn you in?

              JOY

There's that fat Jew for a start.

              TOBY

Nick's not fat. Anyway, what's wrong with Jews?
What the fuck is going on? *(Silence.)* I *believed* in you!

She sneers, turning away from him.

              JOY

Why don't you just piss off.

              TOBY

You know something, Mum? You're evil.

She advances on him. And he's frightened of her. He turns, and goes quickly.

              JOY

              (Calls.)

It's tonight!

ACT TWO

Slight pause. TOBY comes back.

TOBY

What?

JOY smiles.

TOBY

Oh Christ. Where? Who's it going to be? Who's the target?

JOY

Sir Duncan Forbes. KBE.

TOBY

That old fart? What for?

JOY

Strike at the bloody roots! That's what it's for! Marching about with banners? What are *you* good for? Mensheviks, the lot of you.

TOBY

Who's going to do it?

JOY

Who do you think?

He gazes at her, horrified. He thinks she means herself.

JOY

(Dismissive.)

Not me! Ern, of course! Who else has got the bottle? He's *there!* The only revolutionary in the group.

TOBY

(Shakes his head.)

He won't.

JOY

You want to bet?

TOBY

(Shouts, hoarse.)

Call him off!

She smiles. He leaves quickly. She laughs – looking alive and thrilling.

Light change.

ACT TWO SCENE SEVEN

The Café.

TOBY, NICK and PAUL.

NICK

(To TOBY)

Try your place again.

TOBY

I've told you – she's not there.

NICK

D'you think we should ring the police? *(They look at him.)* For Christ's sake, if they're running around with shooters.

PAUL

(To TOBY)

Grass up your old lady? She could end up in Holloway. Try Ern's again.

TOBY

It's half-past seven. Whenever they are -

ACT TWO

NICK

Then we have to do it. Ring him, the old boy they're going to knock off.

TOBY gets up, puts out his hand. They look for change. NICK finds some money.

NICK

Okay, I'll look him up in the book, if he's not listed I'll ring the fuzz – anonymous. I'll do that anyway.
(Counting the money.) There's enough here.

NICK and TOBY go quickly. PAUL sits. CLAIRE enters, sees PAUL, swerves, and crosses to him.

CLAIRE

Hi, you.

PAUL

Where's Joy?

CLAIRE shrugs – she doesn't know.

PAUL

She's got a gun.

CLAIRE

Gun? What ...?

PAUL

They're going to kill somebody.

CLAIRE

Kill? Who?

PAUL
(Irritable.)
I don't know. Some old gink.

CLAIRE

What for?

PAUL

You don't know anything?

CLAIRE

No!

PAUL

What about Ann?

CLAIRE

Ann?

PAUL

Where will I find her?

CLAIRE

Probably down the Community Centre.

He gets up quickly.

PAUL

Can you pay for my coffee?

CLAIRE

Sure.

PAUL

I love you.

CLAIRE

I know.

PAUL

Quick. Do you love me? *(She whispers in his ear.)* What?

CLAIRE

I said I love your cock. Will that do?

ACT TWO

PAUL

Yeah. Dead romantic.

He goes. ERNEST enters, and sees CLAIRE.

ERNEST

Have you seen Joy?

CLAIRE

No I haven't. The boys are looking for her.

ERNEST

Tell them to keep out of it.

CLAIRE

What's going on, Ern?

He gives her a triumphant, baleful glare and goes. NICK enters.

NICK

Where's Paul?

CLAIRE

Looking for Ann in case she knows where Joy is.
Ernie's looking for her too.

NICK

Together?

CLAIRE

No.

NICK

Shit. Toby?

CLAIRE

Haven't seen him.

NICK

We split – to find a 'phone. *(He sits.)* I rang the bloody fuzz.

CLAIRE

What?!

NICK

Anonymously. I said this guy, Sir Duncan Forbes ...

CLAIRE

Who?

NICK

He's the target ... was going to be wasted. Tonight.

CLAIRE

What?

She goes quickly.

NICK

It's okay! I didn't give any names!

JOY enters. NICK freezes. She ignores him as he pulls out a seat for her. She moves the chair away from him, and sits. ERNEST returns, sees JOY and joins her. They talk, heads down. JOY gestures. ERNEST nods. NICK can't sit still. He dodges off.

NICK comes back on – craning his neck, looking for PAUL and TOBY. He smiles weakly when JOY and ERNEST look at him suspiciously.

NICK

I'm waiting for Toby and Paul. We're going to catch a movie. About the Baader-Meinhofs.

They ignore him.

NICK

Worth seeing. Maybe we should have a film section in the group. I know – art section. Books, magazines – films, plays – our own magazine culling the crap. Sell

ACT TWO

it on the street. Get the message out. People need to recognise bourgeois crap for what it is!

They ignore him.

NICK

Where's Scottie? I thought he was ... Weren't you all –? No – got that wrong. That's tomorrow. Premeeting. Advisory group, yeah?

JOY mutters vehemently to ERNEST and rises. NICK panics.

NICK

Toby's looking for you, Joy. He ... There's something ... He's got something for you.

JOY

What?

NICK

He didn't say. He said it was urgent. A message. And he had something – a parcel – for you. He said you'd know what it was.

PAUL and ANN enter. They stop dead at the sight of JOY.

PAUL

Hi Joy. Hi Ern.

JOY

What do you want? *(She makes to go past him. He takes her arm.)* What?

PAUL

I need ... Joy, I need your help. You're the Leader. Ernest, I need to ask Joy's advice. There's no-one else. Ann suggested that I ask you. You're the only sane voice I know.

ANN

Absolutely.

They almost push her into a chair.

JOY

What is it? What do you want?

PAUL

Group solidarity. We can count on you. You're all that stands between us and chaos, Joy. You're the only clear head. We need clarity ...

ANN

Precision.

PAUL

Guidance.

ANN

Now.

PAUL

Urgently. Please. There's a crisis.

JOY

Crisis? What crisis?

PAUL

I – ah ...

JOY

What crisis? Get out of my way! I've better things to do. Don't give me fucking ...

CLAIRE and TOBY enter, arm in arm. JOY, on her feet, glares at them.

ACT TWO

JOY

(To TOBY)

What is it? The message?

TOBY

Message?

JOY

He says – *(Looks at PAUL)* – *(To CLAIRE)* Keep your hands to yourself!

CLAIRE

(Teasing.)

Oooh!

Exaggeratedly, she removes her hand from TOBY's shoulder.

TOBY stares at his mother, defiantly. He puts an arm around CLAIRE. CLAIRE puts an arm around him.

JOY

Get off!

PAUL

(Urgent.)

Claire! Cut it out!

CLAIRE looks at him, grins, then turns, kisses TOBY on the cheek, nuzzling, and lifts a leg around him.

CLAIRE

Coffee, darling?

As she walks away to get coffee, JOY pulls a gun out of her bag, and aims at her. TOBY dives in front of CLAIRE, as she fires.

TOBY takes the bullet – gasps – and makes an odd, stumbling step towards JOY – then falls in front of her.

PAUL leaps forward, lifts TOBY in his arms, and is covered in his blood.

Blackout.

ACT TWO SCENE EIGHT

The House of Commons Committee Room. The Present.

The government meeting is over. Only ANN and PAUL (dressed, and wigged as in the first scene) are left. ANN, perched on the side of the table, is enjoying a cigarette.

ANN

Well...

PAUL

Well!

He bows his head to her, smiling.

PAUL

Good meeting. But will we get anything?

ANN

Yes, I think so. Not as much as you hoped, and not nearly as much as you need.

She closes her briefcase.

PAUL

Busy?

ANN

Oh yes! *(She pauses,)* Do you ever see ... I mean ...

PAUL

See any of the ...?

ACT TWO

ANN

No, well, it's twenty years. *(Slight pause.)* I scarpered.

PAUL

Understandably.

ANN

I was scared, Paul. I didn't want to be shot.

PAUL

You went home?

ANN

I went to Canada. To my cousins. Worked on the farm for a year. Took a couple of degrees – came back – lectured …

PAUL gestures enquiry.

ANN

Politics and economics. Got married to Ian – structural engineer. Three children: Ian, Tom and Sasha. Then there was a call for women candidates, so …

He nods.

PAUL

You were always the hardest worker.

ANN

What happened, Paul? I couldn't even look at a newspaper.

PAUL

It took him two days to die. He was so angry.

ANN groans.

PAUL

She was diagnosed as psychotic.

THE SOCIALISTS

ANN

How on earth could we have...? I believed in her!

PAUL

Yeah.

ANN

Hah! You and Nick were always subversive. What happened to Ernest?

PAUL

Disappeared. Scottie went back to Glasgow. Jim McBride went to sea – till he fell off a boat. He's in A/A now...

ANN

Nick?

PAUL

He's making a fortune in sound systems. Got a manor house in Wales, with geese and miniature ponies for his daughters. His partner designs glassware.

ANN

And Joy? Is Joy still...?

PAUL

Confined? Yes. She's in good health. She writes. Quite well. Her theories would make a lot of sense if you didn't have to apply them to human beings.

ANN

You've read her writings?

PAUL

(Nods)

I visit her.

Silence. She looks up at him.

ACT TWO

ANN

Oh, Paul.

PAUL

He was lovely, Toby. All fixed points – like Joy –but sane. Like an un-cracked bell, a shining hazelnut, full of nutrition. You can't knock off life. It's irreplaceable. The only magic we have. I can't kill an ant.

She leans up, and kisses him. He picks up her briefcase, and helps her on with her jacket.

ANN

I have to be honest, Paul. I'm not mad about slugs.

PAUL

Why? Because they're grey and slimy?

ANN

Yes. And they're squidgy when you tread on them.

PAUL

So, get my amendments through, then we can regenerate the forests. The birds will breed again, and the thrushes can see to the slugs.

ANN laughs.

PAUL

It's really very simple.

They go.

Fade to black.

THE END.

25th AUG – 12th SEPT AT 10pm — A NEW PLAY "GUINEVERE" BY PAM GEMS WITH MAGGIE JORDAN AND SEAN McCARTHY. DIRECTED BY KENNY IRELAND. A FIRST PRODUCTION BY THE SCOTTISH WOMENS COMPANY. KUNDRY'S THEATRE, EDIN WAX MUSEUM 142 HIGH ST.

GUINEVERE

For Trudie Styler

GUINEVERE was first presented by THE SCOTTISH WOMEN'S COMPANY at the Edinburgh Festival Fringe: 25 August–12 September, 1976, at Kundry's Theatre, 142 High Street, Edinburgh with the following cast:

Guinevere	MAGGIE JORDAN
Arthur	SEAN MCCARTHY
Directed by	KENNY IRELAND.
Designed by	TAGO SAKAMOTO
	TETSUO YOSHIMATSU
Lighting designed by	GERRY JENKINSON
Costumes designed by	JEAN SEEL
Production Manager	STEPHEN ORMEROD
Stage Manager	ALISON PEEBLES
Stage Technician	ANDREW DAVENPORT
ASM	SARA GEMS
	CATHERINE EBERHARDIE
	SUE INNES
	PAULA JENNINGS

It was subsequently performed: 11–23 October 1976 at the Soho Poly, Riding House Street, London, with:

Guinevere	ANN MITCHELL
Arthur	TONY SCANNELL
Directed by	CAROLINE EVES
Designed by	DEE GREENWOOD

And presented by the Royal Shakespeare Company: 8–16 March, 1979, at the Gulbenkian Studio, Newcastle, with:

Guinevere	SUZANNE BISHOP
Arthur	CONRAD ASQUITH

REVIEWS.

"There has never been a GUINEVERE like Maggie Jordan who mercilessly berates that arch-chauvinist Arthur, and brings woman's lib to Camelot.

Pam Gems's new play inventively harnesses the legend and has Guinevere pouring out her feelings of desperation and frustration at being treated as chattel by the uncomprehending Arthur, played by Sean McCarthy.

He agrees to make concessions, but she wants more radical change – a redefinition of her role and equal rights with the knights, including a seat on the council.

The clash, during a break in Guinevere's trial for adultery, is well developed, showing up the sham of ingrained attitudes and prejudices.

An auspicious debut for Maggie Jordan's new Scottish Women's Company."

Richard Mowe. *Scottish Evening News*. August 27, 1976

"As playwright Pam Gems and most women know, Hell Hath No Fury Like A Man Scorned. In GUINEVERE, the opening play of the Soho Poly season, King Arthur begs, bullies and threatens his wife so that she will give 'him' (Lancelot) up. In exchange for absolute fidelity, the rapacious King will even grant his wife a degree of political freedom – a seat on the council. Pam Gems's characters may wear medieval costumes of velvet and hair, but their conflicts are horrendous, familiar, and still unresolved. Woman as property, child-bearer, bitch, Goddess – it's the old story cleverly wrought in this 'romantic' version with the contradictions of the female myth sharply exposed. While Pam Gems's play deals with modern and down-to-earth issues, her legendary characters allow her language to be exotic and powerful. Ann Mitchell excels in the title role.

Ann McFerran. *Time Out*. October 15, 1976

GUINEVERE

CHARACTERS

ARTHUR
GUINEVERE
SIR AGRAVAIN
SIR BEDIVERE
LAWYER

GUINEVERE

ACT ONE

ACT ONE SCENE ONE

A raised dais on two levels. A throne on the upper level. Four chairs and a table on the stage level. The setting is magical and Martian – both of war and of the stars. There is a red glow of fire, glinting on weaponry – all set against a starry night.

Throughout the play, which may be played without an interval, the weather, and the time of day, change arbitrarily, fracturing unity.

A pause. The leaping glow of the fire. A LAWYER scurries in, fussing with his many papers.

TWO KNIGHTS enter, and stand behind their chairs. These are SIR AGRAVAIN and SIR BEDIVERE. A pause. Heads turn towards the exit.

At last, ARTHUR enters. He is a huge man, his face scarred and bashed, like a boxer's. His small eyes gleam, jovial but dangerous. On this occasion, he enters without ceremony, and throws himself down on the throne. His body is almost turned away from the proceedings.

SIR AGRAVAINE AND SIR BEDIVERE exchange a glance. They look to ARTHUR, who refuses to catch their eye.

The LAWYER approaches, and SIR AGRAVAIN confers briefly with him. ARTHUR ignores them. SIR BEDIVERE gestures irritably, and the LAWYER presents himself, bowing. ARTHUR growls something inaudible. The KNIGHTS exchange another glance. They decide that permission to proceed has been granted.

SIR AGRAVAIN lifts a gloved hand, giving the signal. A single BELL begins to strike. But OTHER BELLS join in. The noise increases until there is a cacophony – with a GONG, and harsh, high WIND INSTRUMENT sounds. The MEN are forced to put their hands to their ears.

GUINEVERE enters, and the noise ceases. She stands alone, taking her stance, looking wand-like and very fine, her hands clasped before her.

ARTHUR leans forward and squints down at her nastily. The LAWYER hisses urgently at SIR AGRAVAIN. Eventually, ARTHUR drags his eyes from GUINEVERE and nods at the LAWYER.

> ARTHUR
>
> Where were we?

The LAWYER hands ARTHUR a paper. He reads with difficulty.

GUINEVERE smiles, superior. She even holds out her hand for the paper. ARTHUR shoves it under the nose of SIR AGRAVAIN, and they both mutter over it. SIR AGRAVAIN takes over, reading laboriously.

> SIR AGRAVAIN
> *(Reads)*
> "On the occasion of Your Majesty's sojourn in Ireland..."

> ARTHUR
>
> What?

> SIR AGRAVAIN
>
> What?

ACT ONE

ARTHUR

On the occasion of what? Soj? Sir Bedivere. What?

SIR BEDIVERE

When we were beating up the Irish.

ARTHUR

Well, why doesn't it say so! *(All this for Guinevere's benefit.)* Yes ... Right! What about then! I was away a whole year. A whole year, lads! I was away a year!

Murmurs of assent from the KNIGHTS.

ARTHUR

(Bawls to Guinevere, making her flinch.)

Climb out of that one!

He grins at the two knights, with gestures. They bang their fists and feet in support, making a rowdy noise. GUINEVERE smiles a small, superior smile. The LAWYER looks at her humbly for her reply – but none is forthcoming.

ARTHUR

You had a suckler!

LAWYER

(Finding the relevant deposition)

Her Most Sublime Majesty has recorded that the child Engmar was born in the late autumn, after Your Most Gracious Majesty ...

ARTHUR

It was a two-monther! It couldn't even sit up!

LAWYER

Desolate at your absence, Her Most Sublime Majesty ... carried ... ahem ... late. *(He reads:)* "My heart and soul yearned only for the solace of my Lord.

Bereft of his love, I sang to the child within to be my heart's companion until my Lord's return."

ARTHUR

Hah!

GUINEVERE gestures to the LAWYER, who searches in clumsy haste. Eventually, he finds the appropriate paper.

LAWYER

There is a deposition from the midwife, Sire.

ARTHUR

(Disbelieving)

Oh yes ...

LAWYER

(Reads)

"The child's skin was dry, like paper. In the crib, fine strips fell on to his linen. He was wrinkled white from laying too long in the womb. His little nails were an inch long."

As he puts down the paper, GUINEVERE gives a long sigh.

ARTHUR

(Growls)

How late? What does it say?

The LAWYER scans the paper. Speaks quickly and nervously.

LAWYER

The woman says ... two months?

ARTHUR

Cut out her tongue.

SIR AGRAVAIN rises, drawing his sword.

ACT ONE

ARTHUR

Not now, Sir Agravain! Later!

Silence. ARTHUR glowers at GUINEVERE.

ARTHUR

Not – my – child.

GUINEVERE turns her head away, with a superior smile. Then she giggles. It is infectious. The KNIGHTS exchange a smile, and break into laughter. Even the LAWYER smirks.

ARTHUR, at first enraged, decides to join in, and grins, sheepish, making the sign of a cuckold, fingers at temples.

But it all dies away to a heavy silence.

GUINEVERE moves without hurry to the LAWYER. She murmurs in his ear. He tips over the table, looking for a paper. She indicates it with her toe and moves apart. They wait for the LAWYER. He clears his throat, under GUINEVERE's gaze, his hands shaking.

SIR AGRAVAIN

Do you want to say something, man?

LAWYER

We have ... We have presented to us a document.

ARTHUR

Another document?

LAWYER

A ... A deposition, Awesome Majesty.

The KNIGHTS stir. They confer with ARTHUR. We hear the word "confession." ARTHUR lifts his gloved hand.

ARTHUR

Read it.

GUINEVERE

LAWYER

(Nervous)

"It has come to our attention that the Moors, under Your Majesty's command, continue to practice female circumcision."

ARTHUR

Out of order! Out of order!

The LAWYER pauses, but GUINEVERE turns a fearsome face on him, and he continues.

LAWYER

We have here, and are able to present, fifteen witnesses, being females between the ages of nine and seventy. The practice, as we have on sworn oath, is that the female child, on reaching the age of flow, is pinned ritually, and most of the hanging parts are cut away with a piece of sharp glass; the operation taking usually five to seven cuts per side. The two bleeding parts are then rubbed with dirt and thonged together till they have crusted. During this period, the child cries piteously since it is impossible to wet, or to strain, without the most grievous misery. Subsequently, when the child is thirteen, and given in marriage, the husband slits her open for covering. If he leaves her for battle, she may again be sewn, if such be his command.

GUINEVERE stares directly at ARTHUR. They lock eyes.

ARTHUR

(Growls)

Out of order.

GUINEVERE bangs a foot – hard. A ritual sign of displeasure.

ACT ONE

SIR AGRAVAIN

(To Guinevere, respectfully)

It is not germane to the business in hand, Ma'am.

GUINEVERE begins to turn her body rhythmically, this way and that – something between turning and shaking – at the same time giving a soft, sustained hiss. This makes the men uneasy.

SIR BEDIVERE whispers to ARTHUR, who nods.

SIR BEDIVERE

This we will investigate again. It is agreed.

He nods to the LAWYER to proceed with the matter in hand.

LAWYER

Awesome Majesty ... There is a further deposition.

The MEN react with groans and gestures.

ARTHUR

Is it to the point?!

A BELL begins tolling. There is a high wailing offstage.

ARTHUR

Very well – if it's relevant!

The noises cease.

LAWYER

(Finds paper and reads.)

"During the absence of Your Most Royal Majesty in Ireland, twenty-seven cases of rape came before our court ... "

ARTHUR

Be warned!

LAWYER

Your Majesty, I ...

GUINEVERE

He is caught between them. ARTHUR and GUINEVERE both glare at him. He finishes his sentence.

LAWYER

"... twenty-seven cases. In not one case was the defendant found guilty."

He finishes in rapid apology.

LAWYER

Five of the above cases concerned a father violating a member of his own family, usually a daughter. In three cases, the child was under ten years of age. One was a child of six, and one was a child of four.

SIR AGRAVAIN

No, I don't agree with that. No, no.

SIR BEDIVERE

Shame.

LAWYER

(Gaining courage)

We may indeed cry shame, my lords. Of the remaining seventeen cases, eleven were virgins ...

Noises of jovial disbelief from the court.

LAWYER

Three were married women ...

He consults his papers.

LAWYER

One was accosted as she carried a pail of milk and was set upon by *(Consults paper)* nine men. She has since died. They trod upon her pelvis. One was raped by her brother-in-law in the seventh month of pregnancy and brought forth a dead child. And

ACT ONE

the third cannot speak of it, but bleeds and shakes.
Of the remainder, one was a widow in her sixtieth
year; another likewise was a crone, who smiles and
chuckles. The last is a whore.

A burst of laughter. As the laughter subsides ...

LAWYER
The contention of the deposition is that even a whore
may have the currency of her on body within her
choosing in a realm which claims order within its
boundaries.

SIR BEDIVERE
But the women have been told to carry knives.

SIR AGRAVAIN
Jewelled pins. Or pepper for the eyes.

The LAWYER makes a plaintive gesture towards GUINEVERE, who gives him a sardonic look.

LAWYER
My lords ... My lords, I have here depositions from
witnesses who tried to oppose their attackers, as
suggested. In the main, their injuries have been more
extensive since the men, angered by resistance, have,
in each case, inflicted further punitive injuries upon
them. The women now fear to report rape at all.

GUINEVERE approaches the dais, challenging ARTHUR to respond. He glowers at her; turns away, thinking, and makes his decision.

ARTHUR
It is not the time nor the place. This matter will be
dealt with where it is relevant. You are out of order,
and you show contempt for these proceedings. We

ask ourselves why you seek to divert us with these
matters. *(He masters his rage.)* Continue.

GUINEVERE moves apart.

> SIR AGRAVAIN
>
> *(Getting out his notes)*
>
> Ye-es – well now. *(He clears his throat.)* It was agreed
> that, when we went campaigning ... even on the
> Quest ...

ARTHUR lifts a warning hand.

> SIR AGRAVAIN
>
> Sorry, Sire, but I am under oath. The fact is, it does
> go on. I mean, we men ... Well, put it this way. When
> I kicked off, my father introduced me to a very nice
> foreign lady ...

Laughter.

> SIR AGRAVAIN
>
> A nice, respectable, married lady from a good family.
> Older than me, of course. That was how things were
> done, after all. If I'd gone to a whorehouse, ten to one
> I'd have got the pox. You all know what I'm talking
> about.

> ARTHUR
>
> Go on, sir knight.

> SIR AGRAVAIN
>
> Let's face it, we all started off this way. It's a
> very civilised arrangement. Husbands away on
> campaigns; wives lonely. Well, my point is – this sort
> of arrangement, well, it could hardly work without
> the ... ah, well ... without the cooperation of ladies of
> a decent sort. What I mean to say is ...

ACT ONE

ARTHUR

Whose side are you on, Agravain?

SIR AGRAVAIN

Just trying to be fair, Your Majesty.

SIR BEDIVERE

You mean: don't get caught!

Brief laughter from the court. Even the LAWYER smiles.

ARTHUR

You mean, if you're the woman, don't get caught?
One standard for the men, one for the women? Is that
what you're saying, Agravain?

SIR AGRAVAIN

How can we deny it, Sire? 'Tis the natural order
of things. Must have our ladies chaste. With the
servants, it's different, of course. Though, even there,
it's hard kicking the poor little things out of doors
when their bellies swell. Half the time it's your own
flesh and blood they're carrying. Still, must keep
things regular. And they *will* come sidling up to a
man, all fresh and shining, showing off their little
high bosoms. Not that I stand for rape. No. No need to
go forcing girls. Not unless you're really desperate. A
bunch of flowers. A few sweetmeats. That's what I tell
the young squires. As for what the heathens do with
their women, Ma'am, afraid I can't help you there.
I've had Moorish women in my time and it's true.
Some of them are all scarred up. Very passive sort of
creatures. Some men like that, of course.

GUINEVERE

Having lost his way, SIR AGRAVAIN sits abruptly. SIR BEDIVERE rises. ARTHUR squints at him warily. GUINEVERE turns away with a sweeping motion.

> SIR BEDIVERE
>
> We must keep to the point. The charges are grave. The penalties severe. A forced entry ... a mishap ... a single fall from grace through drink, or weakness, melancholy even ... Forgiveness ... (*Bowing towards the King.*) Forgiveness would be seen as the proper mercy of the strong towards the weak. But what we have here is an accusation of a different order. If the charges, or any one of the charges here presented is proved beyond reasonable doubt, then the penalties are clearly laid down. To wit: First – mutilation. Second – breaking on a wheel. Third – garroting. Fourth – quartering, with the head to be displayed on the palace gate till it be picked clean by the crows, then crushed under a stone until only fragments remain to be strewn outside the boundary of the realm.

Silence. ARTHUR fidgets, tapping with something. He continues to tap. Then he stops.

> SIR BEDIVERE
>
> We come to the question of offspring.

> ARTHUR
>
> What? Offspring?

> SIR BEDIVERE
>
> If illegitimacy is proven, Sire, they will have to be put to the sword.

Silence.

ACT ONE

SIR AGRAVAIN

You are speaking, Sir Knight, of the end of a dynasty.
His Majesty has no brothers nor other kith.

SIR BEDIVERE

I seek only to emphasize the significance of the
finding of this court, given the implication of the
charges.

He sits. ARTHUR grimaces.

LAWYER

(Rising)

It is not, I think, in the ... ah ... indictment implied
that *all* of the royal princes are ...

SIR BEDIVERE

Is there specification?

LAWYER

Ah ... no. But ...

SIR BEDIVERE

You imply that among the five royal sons, that one, at
least, is legitimate.

LAWYER

Oh yes, absolutely.

SIR BEDIVERE

Which one?

LAWYER

I beg your pardon?

SIR BEDIVERE

Which one? We need to know. It is a matter of rightful
inheritance. The sanctity of the marriage bed may be
of little importance to women. Why should they care?

GUINEVERE

They never inherit responsibility. What is a woman but a reflection of the husband who chooses her? The father whose dowry defines her? In the olden days, what matter who got a woman's belly up, so long as there were boys to drive the herd, and girls to spin? But now we have emerged from incoherence, from the spontaneity of pasture, from the dangers of the random. Those times have gone.

GUINEVERE, her back to us, moves slightly.

SIR BEDIVERE

People died, of hunger, of drought! From rock-fall, flood, the bludgeon of the marauder! But no more. Here, in this kingdom, we have order. No more tribal wanderings. Instead – we till, we crop, we husband! We build bridges, build dykes, strongholds, towns where guildsmen and crafts may flourish. Our granaries are full for the long winter. Our animals survive. When, in this kingdom, did a woman last lose her milk for want of sustenance? Do you expect all this for nothing, madam?

SIR AGRAVAIN

He's right! A man ties himself down. Gives up his freedom – which isn't natural for a man. Oh, they're all silks and sighs when the halter's out for you. Soon as they're breeding, we're in the way! Don't want it! No, keep a woman in her place, I say. Same as a dog. 'Course, you have to do your duty in the bed or they get vicious. But you mustn't let them take you for granted. Keep them on the hop. A few little surprises now and then. Women like a moody man. They get bored. Not surprising really. Still, we made the world.

ACT ONE

It's up to them to fit in, eh? And keep 'em up to the
mark. Believe me, they're happier for it. Not that I'm
not fond of the little beggars. They can twist their way
round ...

SIR BEDIVERE

This is too personal. The matter is simple. For the
good order of the state, inheritance must be secure
and thus the marriage bed inviolate. A woman knows
that what comes out of her belly is her own. *Can we
ever be sure?*

He sits. Silence.

ARTHUR

Madam? Have you nothing to say? No answer?

GUINEVERE inclines her head slightly and her LAWYER crosses to
her side. She whispers to him, gesticulating slightly. The LAWYER
returns to his position.

LAWYER

Your Majesty ... honoured knights. Her Majesty
humbly requests reply to her depositions.

ARTHUR leans down, confers with the KNIGHTS. They press him
to conduct the interrogation.

ARTHUR

The court ... The court considers that these are mere
tactics. Irrelevancies.

LAWYER

Awesome Majesty, perhaps we should make allowance
for the sex of the ... ah ... defendant. Her Majesty is
ill-acquainted with ...

GUINEVERE

ARTHUR

She can stay on the point well enough when the
matter is to her advantage! Stand aside. These
immaterial statements, what do they amount to?
Incest? You know I'm against that – weakens the
stock. As for rape, who breeds these monsters? Who
has them to heel as pups? Women. Not the men.
Before you bring your accusations, look to yourselves.
If you have witnesses, call them. Otherwise, this
court will proceed to judgement. You are accused of
high treason. The charge is adultery. Betrayal of your
husband ... your lover ... your king. It is alleged that
you have ... exposed yourself ... the secrets of your
body ... that you, my wife, the Queen ...

He sits, head bowed. As he recovers himself, GUINEVERE makes a move forward. But the LAWYER prevents her from approaching him. He looks up and regards her bleakly.

ARTHUR

How could you do this? Why? Have you no witnesses?
Is there no-one to prove your innocence? To defend
you?

Silence.

SIR BEDIVERE

Here we see the reality. When we remove the
husband, the woman is truly alone. Here we see,
naked, the arrogant foolishness which can lead only
to self-destruction. We see guilt and irresponsibility.
This woman has reneged on herself, on her central
responsibility to those whom she has created –
her children – and on her protector. She seeks
to dispossess he by whose generosity she has

ACT ONE

been enriched. She has knowingly, and willfully, disenthroned herself.

ARTHUR

Not one witness! Not one?

GUINEVERE gestures to the LAWYER. He sighs.

ARTHUR

Well?

LAWYER

Your Majesty...

ARTHUR

Well?

LAWYER

(Shakes his head)

I am instructed...

SIR BEDIVERE

Get on with it.

LAWYER

Her Majesty instructs me... I speak as instructed... *(He looks at GUINEVERE but she is motionless.)* I am instructed to call on behalf of the defence... the air... the water... the earth... and that which grows thereon... the lady moon... and the cave of dream.

SIR BEDIVERE

Rubbish.

SIR AGRAVAIN

Oh dear.

ARTHUR

Have you finished?

GUINEVERE

The LAWYER looks to GUINEVERE again. She nods.

LAWYER

Her ... Her Majesty would like them to be heard.

ARTHUR

Very well. Call the first witness.

LAWYER

I call ... on behalf of her Most Royal Majesty, Queen Guinevere ... the air.

He sits down, defeated.

ARTHUR

Has he been sworn?

LAWYER

(Bobbing up)

Majesty?

ARTHUR

Has the witness been sworn?

LAWYER

Majesty, I ... Sir, I command you to tell the truth, and only the truth before the Lion of Pendragon, Arthur, Great King of all England.

Pause.

ARTHUR

What has the air to say? The air is silent. The witness declines to testify. Speak up! *(A roar.)* Nothing? Is the prisoner an adulteress or no? You are a material witness. When the crime occurred, you were present!

Pause.

ACT ONE

ARTHUR

The witness declines to answer. Tell him to stand down and, for silence, read consent. Is that not the law? Your witness turns against you, madam. You have chosen badly. *(To the LAWYER.)* If there are witnesses with eyes and ears and tongues, let them come forth. No-one? No-one at all? Where's your magic now? Where's Merlin? Got the wind up? They've all deserted you. I've never seen you look so plain. What's the matter? Were you expecting your lover to ride up on a white charger and carry you off? If so, you have made a serious misjudgment. Your lover has spoken for the prosecution. Show her the document.

He hands the document to the LAWYER, who presents it to GUINEVERE. She glances down at it briefly, closes her eyes and sways. The LAWYER holds her.

LAWYER

Her Majesty is faint.

ARTHUR

Move an adjournment.

GUINEVERE clutches the LAWYER's sleeve. They confer.

LAWYER

Your Majesty ... my lords. Her Majesty is ready to speak.

KNIGHTS

Ah! Aahah!

ARTHUR looks down at GUINEVERE in alarm.

ARTHUR

You want to speak?

GUINEVERE

No reply.

ARTHUR

Are you sure it will be in your interest?

SIR BEDIVERE

If Her Majesty is prepared to make a statement ...

ARTHUR

Do you know what you are doing? If you need more time ...

GUINEVERE shakes her head.

ARTHUR

Very well. If you are sure that you are ready.

SIR AGRAVAIN

Oh, let her speak, man. Let her speak.

ARTHUR

No, wait.

SIR BEDIVERE

The accused must answer the charges.

The LAWYER makes to approach her, but she lifts a hand. They wait.

GUINEVERE

I ... I ... I cannot ...

It looks as if ARTHUR will rise, but the KNIGHTS turn to him and he resumes his seat.

GUINEVERE

You ... I ...

LAWYER

(Whispers)

My lady ...

ACT ONE

GUINEVERE

(After a slight pause)

You have confined me. You have confined me. *(Pause)* You have committed violence upon me. Let me try to explain. *(Pause)* When I came into prison, I understood that you were angry with me. That I would not see my children. It was made plain to me that I had incurred displeasure. Why did you not explain the nature of the damage that you intended to inflict upon me? *(Slight pause.)* You ask me for a statement ... Deposition ... For confession. For witnesses. An account of occurrences ... Happenings ... Meetings ... Confession of unacceptable conjunction ... Co-habitation ... Assignation. Rumours ... Murmurs ... Reports of wild gossip ... Innuendo. What, after all, happened?

Pause.

ARTHUR

Get on. Get on with it!

GUINEVERE

When I came into prison, I brought my linen. Only the simpler garments, of course. I was even curious. It was, after all, a new experience. A queen should understand the exigencies of her people. There might even have been a book about it. A lyric. A lay to be sung in the Marches. After all, I was guilty.

ARTHUR

Guilty?!

KNIGHTS

Guilty?!

GUINEVERE

To have been so warm, so well fed. To have had tables ... Chairs ... an ivory bed. My babies in the finest silk. Servants to take away the piss. It was never like that at home. At home, we ...

ARTHUR

We know what you came from.

GUINEVERE

I even hoped for a rest ... From pressure. Importunate friends ... Beggars. Intriguers. Advisers. Those with something to sell. Charms. A new love-apple. German alliance. Oh, those cradle weddings! Most of all, my ear, as trade wind to the King ... Arthur. The leader. The monarch. Source of all power. Decision. I needed a rest from influence. *(Slight pause.)* A small cell perhaps. White painted. With touches of blue. Just a crucifix. And books of an improving nature. Perhaps a poem or two. A rest. Respite. From the clamour of the nursery. An opportunity for self-examination. Was one at fault? Something more grave than irritability? Dissonance. The rub of time wearing rims between us? *(Slight pause.)* You were allowed to walk in the courtyard, late in the afternoon. After the sun had gone in. *(Pause.)* They gave me writing paper. Pens. I try to write. Ahh! No, quick, put it away before they come. To speak is to kill. Do and say nothing. The paper crackles. Yes, I understand. And all the while the brain, you see, is like a dried raisin in a shoebox. There are maggots in my head. Click beetles. Woodlice. Earwigs. Who is that drumming? No, no, it isn't me. Where is the noise coming from? It's louder

ACT ONE

than a regiment! Tomorrow I shall write to my father. Of course! Why didn't I think of that before? He will protect me. Savages! There is a Catherine wheel between my shoulder blades. A flat disc of fire. Who put it there? Could you leave the door open please? I am willing to stop screaming. I know how tiresome it must be. If you would just leave the door slightly ajar. There is no question of my leaving. I've given my word. In any case, where would I go? *(Slight pause.)* Ah! Now I understand! I am trapped. In ice. Perhaps they threw me down a well ... That's why my legs are so stiff. Doctor, my legs are brittle, I can't bend them. Would you send me a doctor, please? I can't bend my legs. They give you liquid paraffin. And if that doesn't work. An enema. The worst thing of all is the vertigo. The wobble. It's bound to make you feel sick. Nauseated. You can't expect the body to react otherwise. Obviously. Obviously. Obviously.

ARTHUR

What?

GUINEVERE

You fall down. *(Pause.)* Of course, we ran very wild out there on the marsh. I didn't wear shoes until I was fourteen. That's why my feet are so broad. *(Smiles)* Broad feet are fashionable now. Not that these matters are significant one way or the other. Sometimes the air is full of wheat chaff. I can't breathe! They are trying to suffocate me! I'm choking in the dust. They're clever. Cleverer than they seem! It's devilish. If they want to kill me, why not a noose? Poison. No. This is too cruel. Is this, after all, a cruel country? I have decided to hit the walls with the flat

of my hand. Go over every inch ... hard. I shall soon
get results. Washing down the walls with moisture
will remove the dust. And the blood will brighten
the cell. No. Don't do that, don't do that. Where are
the hours? Oh God ... Please God ... Now the cell's
moving again. I'm sorry, was that my voice? There
is a man singing outside. Could you have it stopped,
please? There – you see? It's flown away again. I can't
think. What are you doing? Please take no notice of
what I say. They're putting words into my mouth. In
any case, I haven't signed. I would have signed. Just
to get some sleep. I could always have repudiated
the statement. The signature was unacceptable.
Inauthentic. My hand trembled too much. No, thank
you. I'm not hungry. Who's that? Who's out there? If
only I didn't have this headache. I need competent
medical help. Just some civilised cooperation in a
situation that is difficult for us all. Please ... No, don't
do that ... Don't do that. Don't do that. No ... No ...
Please ... I ... I ...

Silence.

SIR AGRAVAIN

It's quite clear to me the lady's not fit to plead!

GUINEVERE

Did I just say something? I have been imprisoned, not
because of adultery, but because I am a woman.

Slight pause.

SIR BEDIVERE

She returns to accusation.

ACT ONE

LAWYER
(To ARTHUR)

My Lord ... My lady is ill.

ARTHUR
(He is upset.)

It seems so. The rigours of prison have been too great for her.

SIR AGRAVAIN

We must be merciful, Sire.

SIR BEDIVERE

The state requires, first, justice.

ARTHUR

But if she's not fit to plead?

SIR AGRAVAIN

What's to be done?

ARTHUR

Withdrawal from the court, perhaps, to a safe place.

LAWYER

To Hereford, Sire. The air is sweet there, and the country beautiful. Recovery there ...

SIR BEDIVERE

We are here to pronounce sentence on crime.

SIR AGRAVAIN

But if the lady is sick?

SIR BEDIVERE

A verdict must be made. The state will not wait. The question of the succession ...

GUINEVERE

ARTHUR

Hereford for the time being. These matters can be adjourned...

SIR BEDIVERE

And the woman retires to a palace!

LAWYER

If that be not agreeable to your lordships, perhaps the Abbey of Crewe? The nuns there are...

GUINEVERE

The Abbey of Crewe? With those old witches? Shut your foolish mouth.

SIR BEDIVERE

Not so sick now, madam... hey?

GUINEVERE, furious with the LAWYER, sets about him, clouting him over the head.

GUINEVERE

Do you think I pay you in good gold coin to have me packed off to the crows? You've no more wit than your wall-eyed mother.

The KNIGHTS attempt to pull her off the LAWYER. She turns on them, screeching and flailing.

SIR BEDIVERE

Would you?

SIR AGRAVAIN

Madam... Madam...

GUINEVERE

Take your foul, stinking hands from me... I read the death in your eyes.

ACT ONE

SIR AGRAVAIN

Madam, please ... It ill becomes you.

GUINEVERE

Get off, you old fool. Rapist!

SIR AGRAVAIN

Now, that's not fair.

But SIR BEDIVERE grabs her firmly.

SIR BEDIVERE

This is a court of law, madam. There are some of us who will not see the law brought into disrepute.

GUINEVERE

For which you would kill, not just me, not just my children, my babe in arms ... But ...

SIR BEDIVERE

Control yourself!

GUINEVERE

I read his eyes. I read his eyes! Death. Death! Not my death. Yours! Yours. Yours!

She screeches at ARTHUR.

GUINEVERE

They will kill you! They want you dead! I read their envy. I read their lust. I read their hate! Hate! Hate!

She buffets the LAWYER aside. He falls. She approaches SIR BEDIVERE. He backs off, intimidated. Then, cornered, draws his sword.

GUINEVERE

SIR BEDIVERE

She's a witch! Kill her! Kill her! In the name of the Table! In the name of Law and Order ... of the Constitution!

GUINEVERE

Touch me and you won't live to see your son's faces again.

SIR BEDIVERE

Draw your sword, man! Before she witches the life from your skull. Adulteress! Whore!

GUINEVERE makes to flee. But SIR AGRAVAIN blocks her way.

GUINEVERE

Move, you old fool! Kill me, would you? You couldn't catch a duck on a pond!

She evades him. But the LAWYER, scurrying to escape, crosses her path and she trips over him. SIR BEDIVERE grabs her by the hair and pulls back her head, exposing her throat.

SIR BEDIVERE

Die, you witch!

As he raises his sword, ARTHUR gives a terrifying roar; leaps down into the arena, slashes at SIR BEDIVERE, wounding him, and picks up GUINEVERE.

He makes off with her.

Blackout.

END OF ACT ONE

ACT TWO

ACT TWO SCENE ONE

The Queen's Bedchamber.

It is light, with gauzes. Simple. Near to Nature. There is a pool. And a fire – and the Queen's Throne – silver, ornate, without arms. A door slams, loud. And another, louder and closer.

GUINEVERE enters, in a rage. Her wrists are bound in a fine thong. We hear the doors bang again as ARTHUR approaches. GUINEVERE hides her anger. By the time ARTHUR enters, she is an odalisque.

ARTHUR bursts in and makes as if to attack her. But she glares at him. They walk about, both of them enraged and dangerous.

ARTHUR

(Mutters.)

When she does open her mouth – totally off the point!

GUINEVERE

What? What are you chewing? If you must chew something, chew fennel! At least it's good for your stomach!

ARTHUR

There's nothing wrong with my stomach.

GUINEVERE

Your paunch, you mean!

They circle each other, glaring.

ARTHUR

(Mutters.)

At least I'm not constipated.

GUINEVERE

I see. You've been having my stools examined.

ARTHUR

(Heavy sarcasm.)

They were, of course, scented.

Both still moving.

GUINEVERE

My God, what a farce.

They cross.

ARTHUR

I'm glad you find it so, madam.

ACT TWO

GUINEVERE

Glad? What do you mean? You're not glad, so why say it? You talk nonsense, the lot of you!

ARTHUR

You find the Council nonsense?

GUINEVERE

So do you when it suits you. As for being off the point ...

ARTHUR

I would earnestly advise you, madam, to take the findings of this court very seriously. What was all that rubbish about? Do you think you can fool them with that? They know very well you've been having food sent in ... your dressmakers ... Whole prison smelt like a French howdedo. See how you feel when you've been in irons twenty years.

GUINEVERE

Oh, don't be such a bully. And stop calling me madam.

ARTHUR

Better than most of the names they call you. *(She looks at him sharply.)* Filthy names behind your back!

GUINEVERE

Oh, behind my back.

ARTHUR

In my hearing.

GUINEVERE

And you put up with it? You fool, they wouldn't do that in front of me. No wonder they think you're getting soft. Take this off!

GUINEVERE

She displays her bound wrists.

ARTHUR

Sorry, not in my jurisdiction.

GUINEVERE

Get it off. Get it off, you bastard, or I'll scratch your face. Get it off!

ARTHUR

Oh, for Christ's sake! Do you want them all to hear?

He cuts her bonds with a fearful-looking knife.

GUINEVERE

It's all very well for you. Look! *(She displays her wrists.)* Tying me up! What sort of games do you think you're playing?

ARTHUR

Playing? Oh, we're not playing games. *(He looks at her bleakly.)* You can disabuse yourself of that.

GUINEVERE

You mean you want me murdered. You want your wife murdered? The mother of your children murdered? Is that what you want?

He does not reply.

GUINEVERE

Is that what you want? *(He still does not reply.)* Where would that leave you?

ARTHUR

It would leave me without an adulteress for a queen.

GUINEVERE

Oh well, if you sit about listening to gossip ...

ACT TWO

ARTHUR

Since the accusations against you have been proved and documented, not to mention what I've been forced to witness with my own eyes, you stand there a liar within your own mouth.

He suddenly groans and collapses. Sits heavily.

ARTHUR

What can I...? We started so high. We were strong. Beautiful. Well-born. What could we do but aim for the highest? Anything less would have been irresponsible. We agreed. We agreed to put in everything. Justify the blind chance of our privilege.

She fidgets with her clothing.

ARTHUR

And now what? What is there for our children but the very decadence we swore to overthrow? You knew my aims, my hopes ... even my weaknesses. I held nothing back. I trusted you. You could do what you liked with me. You alone! You alone had that privilege. And you've destroyed me with it.

GUINEVERE

Don't be such a fool.

ARTHUR

Yes, it was foolish.

He looks across at her, genuinely curious.

ARTHUR

Has loyalty no value to you? None at all?

GUINEVERE
(Thinks, then)
About as much as consistency.

ARTHUR
So, everything I've told you has been at risk?

GUINEVERE
I've used my own judgment.

He towers over her, in a terrifying fury.

ARTHUR
And who said you could do that?

She cowers, trembling. He notices this and it disconcerts him.

ARTHUR
Now what are you doing? What are you shaking for?

GUINEVERE
(In a small voice.)
Stop shouting. You're always shouting. I don't like it.

ARTHUR
(Sitting)
Oh, for God's sake, what am I supposed to do? *(He fumes.)* To be brought down by a woman!

GUINEVERE
Yes. A woman. That nothing.

ARTHUR
I didn't mean...

GUINEVERE
Yes, you did. Poor you. No wonder they're laughing. Well, it's worse than breaking your neck tripping over your own dog.

ACT TWO

ARTHUR

What are you on about? I've always respected you! As Arthur's queen you've held an unrivalled and impregnable position of influence and dignity.

GUINEVERE

Oh, Arthur's queen! Guinevere. Arthur's queen. Guinevere. Arthur's wife. Guinevere, mother of princes. Guinevere – daughter of the Lame King ...

She turns on him, becoming the goddess.

GUINEVERE

Guinevere – Queen of the Orchard. Guinevere – Queen of The Moon. Guinevere – Queen of the Water. Guinevere – Queen of the Sun!

ARTHUR blenches, but recovers quickly.

ARTHUR

Any position you hold is by my dispensation.

GUINEVERE

As you so often see fit to remind me.

ARTHUR

I never remind you.

GUINEVERE

You remind me constantly.

ARTHUR

I've never rubbed it in. I've always shared everything. You say yourself how generous I am.

GUINEVERE

It hasn't occurred to you that your benevolence might be stifling?

GUINEVERE

ARTHUR

I've never seen you hang back.

GUINEVERE

Oh, you like to give. You enjoy it. You do it very well. I don't mean stylishly. It's usually fished out of your back pocket. But you never come empty-handed. Why?

ARTHUR

Why?

GUINEVERE

Why? Why presents all the time?

ARTHUR

Why? Because I love you, that's why!

GUINEVERE

But why do I need presents? Why do I need presents?

ARTHUR

I thought so. Here it comes.

GUINEVERE

You know very well! I've had claustrophobia since the day I married you!

ARTHUR

Claustrophobia? You can't even spell the word!

GUINEVERE

Neither can you. Acute claustrophobia – and agoraphobia. I'm afraid to go out. I'm afraid to stay in. I spend my life on the stoop. What sort of life is that?

ARTHUR

It's your nerves! It happens with women!

ACT TWO

GUINEVERE

Oh, it happens.

ARTHUR

Yes, well, as I say ...

GUINEVERE

Because we're so weak, no doubt. Feeble. Not up to it. Second-rate. Number two. Do you never wonder why we're so miserable in the great world you've created for us? You think it can be cured with amethysts? I never wear the sapphires. They give me migraine. As for those dumpy bracelets, they can go back to the Danes as far as I'm concerned.

ARTHUR

Oh, they can, can they? That's easier said than done. They cost me half an ear!

GUINEVERE

Just to give me a rash, all up my arms. Look!

ARTHUR

(Growls.)

There's nothing wrong with your arms. They're white as milk.

GUINEVERE

I found a cure.

ARTHUR

(Grim)

You found a cure all right.

GUINEVERE

You should be pleased. Not so much silver finding its way to Merlin's back door.

ARTHUR

Bloody quack. Oh, spend what you want. Live on chickweed and tadpoles. *I'm* telling you it's your nerves.

GUINEVERE

(After a slight pause)

At least it's better than heartburn. Why don't you follow the Eastern masters, as Merlin says? You wouldn't be so tense!

ARTHUR

And if they weren't tense, they wouldn't have had to dream up yoga in the first place, poor starving bastards. As usual, you've managed to get me off the subject.

He moderates his voice – going for a more reasonable approach.

ARTHUR

This adjournment is for you to put your case. Then I'll present you in the best possible light.

GUINEVERE

Adjournment? Adjournment? They were trying to kill me!

ARTHUR

I must appear impartial.

GUINEVERE

Impartial. Hah!

ARTHUR

And what were you doing?!

He realizes he is shouting, and lowers his voice.

ACT TWO

ARTHUR

What was all that gibberish? I told you what to do –
say nothing, look at the floor, wear something simple.
And you come looking like that! I do my best, and you
throw the game away.

GUINEVERE

The game.

ARTHUR

I told you the depositions would get up their nostrils.
It's neither the time nor the place. Then we get the
amateur dramatics.

GUINEVERE

Thank you.

ARTHUR

And, to top it all, you set about your own lawyer!
What was the point of that? Just tell me!

GUINEVERE

He's a fool.

ARTHUR

Very helpful.

GUINEVERE

You're all fools!

ARTHUR

Look. Look, we must try and work together. I'm
trying to help you. How can I help you if you won't
help yourself?

She doesn't respond.

GUINEVERE

ARTHUR

At least try. Try to concentrate. I'll help you. You, of all people, must be seen to have justice ... must have justice.

She gives a little smile at the slip. He moves, awkward.

ARTHUR

Would you like to make a statement? *(No reply)* You've had ample time to prepare your case ... waivers ... adjournments ... We've all fallen over backwards. We've listened to all your ...

He pauses.

ARTHUR

(Lowers voice)

The other ... party has even offered to withdraw.

She turns, her face altering.

GUINEVERE

(Harsh)

No! There'll be none of that!

ARTHUR

What?

GUINEVERE

Picking him off as soon as he's outside the castle walls!

ARTHUR

You don't really think I'd do that, do you?

GUINEVERE

(Slight pause)

Perhaps not you. Others might, to please you.

ACT TWO

ARTHUR

If they did, I'd have their heads for it.

GUINEVERE

(Dry)

Very helpful. Like the time my dog was killed and you brought me a man's head on a plate, swimming in blood.

ARTHUR

You laughed! You thought it was funny!

GUINEVERE

Only because I was terrified. The blood ran up my sleeves.

Pause.

ARTHUR

You must present your case. *(Pause.)* You must say something.

GUINEVERE

(Bursts out)

You've been unfaithful to me enough times!

ARTHUR

(Genuinely surprised.)

That's different! You don't expect a man ... A man can't be satisfied with one woman. Law of nature.

GUINEVERE

I agree.

ARTHUR

You do? Ah, but then you would, wouldn't you? It suits your case. *(Pause.)* I was away a lot. I missed you.

GUINEVERE

What about me? I missed *you*.

ARTHUR

You had the children.

GUINEVERE

Oh, I see. I'm supposed to suck my sons off.

ARTHUR

Stop that!

GUINEVERE

(Flinching at his bellow)

What?

ARTHUR

Why do you do it? Foul-mouthed. Coarse. You know I don't care for it.

GUINEVERE

(Dry)

No, your privilege that.

She struts about like a man, leering and winking, shaping a bottom with her hand. tapping the side of her nose, clenching her fist suggestively, nudging and goosing him, and making kissing noises.

ARTHUR

Have you gone mad?

GUINEVERE

Oho! Can't have that, can we? The goddess, farting? The Myth, picking her nose. The Ineffable Mother – pissing in the alley? No, no. Having been graced with the honour of chalicing *you* into life, we must, naturally, be divine! Hah!

For once, she makes him jump.

ACT TWO

GUINEVERE

You were so green you didn't even know that what we did together made our son! All those draughty temples covered in bird lime ... Great fat-bellied idols with dead flowers and rotting oranges! When I finally convinced you, we never heard the end of it. Your whang was into everything that moved.

ARTHUR

Can you not see that this sort of talk merely erodes my respect for you?

GUINEVERE

Debases the currency, you mean? Devalues the property?

ARTHUR

You weren't always like this. As a girl, you were very quiet. Reserved. The first time we met you didn't even open your mouth.

GUINEVERE

I was trying not to faint. Even my father put down his pint. And the parrot was so scared, he fell off my arm.

ARTHUR

Shut up.

GUINEVERE

Well, you stank! Ugh!

ARTHUR

I'd just clawed my way up a cliff face for you! Bloody tentacles! Every time you chopped the things, they spat black blood. I was drenched in the stuff.

GUINEVERE

It was in your hair for days.

ARTHUR

And all that after a year on a dark sea. No wind in the sails, just a blinding fog. Constant hissing. Shining fins and eyes – and nothing. Nothing to eat! When we slid on to that shore, it was littered with bird carcasses, shrivelled dry. No trees. No life.

GUINEVERE

You didn't look like men at all. I'm not surprised they tried to see you off.

ARTHUR

That's right. I had to choke a man at the gate.

GUINEVERE

My father's falconer. A fine start.

ARTHUR

I apologised!

GUINEVERE

Apologised? You fell asleep during the speeches! Not to mention the rest of your behaviour that night.

ARTHUR

What was I supposed to do? You sat there in that yellow thing with a prim look on your face, and your hand on your thigh ...

GUINEVERE

I had a flea up my skirt!

ARTHUR

We-ell, what was I supposed to do?

GUINEVERE

What you were supposed to do was kiss my hand, not jump me. They nearly broke it off there and then.

ACT TWO

ARTHUR

Ah, cunning old bastard, your father. He saw how the land lay. He'd already had a whole fleet and half a country off me. What more did he want?

GUINEVERE

You also slept with my mother.

ARTHUR

Oh, yes, well, I wasn't used to the brand of liquor.

GUINEVERE

She couldn't walk for a week.

ARTHUR

Well, she should have stood in the light.

GUINEVERE

And what was all that about your mother? I never knew whether to believe it or not.

He looks at her with an odd, blank-eyed look.

ARTHUR

(Easily)

The old tigress. That was rage. She'd have kept her hands on me if she could. I soon cleared out of that one. Kicked her in the bladder, and rode my horse over her.

GUINEVERE

I see. So, you stepped on her and rode away.

ARTHUR

I was looking for you. For love.

GUINEVERE

Love? Love? That old witch would have died for you. She smelt the axe often enough – perjuring herself.

251

Love? Men don't love. Oh, they feel affection. Desire.
But love? We love. By God, we even love your ugliness.
Do you love ours? When does a man love an ugly
woman? But we love you because we love first, desire
after. When have you looked at an ugly woman?

ARTHUR

Many times.

GUINEVERE

When it was all you could get. *(Pause.)* No. You don't
love me. If you loved me, you'd defend me. Right or
wrong.

ARTHUR

Even when the wrong's against me?

GUINEVERE

I've forgiven you enough times.

ARTHUR

That's different. Nothing I've ever done has
threatened you. I've protected you. What you're
seeking to do is destroy me. Your actions undo all my
work. You appear to wish to obliterate me – to show
me up as weak, or of consequence; to put your foot in
my face and paddle in the ruin. No! I do not permit
this. I perceive and I do not permit. If necessary . . . if
necessary, I shall do what has to be done. So, be aware
of that.

GUINEVERE

As I say, you don't love me.

An appreciable pause.

ARTHUR

You're my life. I know that.

ACT TWO

GUINEVERE

Am I?

ARTHUR

You know you are. You're part of me.

GUINEVERE

Belly and all? (*Laughs.*) By God! The first time you heard me howl, you were off to that chapel praising the Lord you'd been born a man. The whole palace heard you throw up.

ARTHUR

I couldn't bear to see you suffer!

GUINEVERE

Ye-es. You were so soft-hearted that, while I was in labour for three days, you chased yellow-haired laundresses through the yards.

ARTHUR

Now, don't bring all that up …

GUINEVERE

By God, when they wiped the sweat off my face, I couldn't even cry out, lest they should think it was for that!

ARTHUR

You said you wouldn't bring it up.

GUINEVERE

And what happened when I put him to suck for you? You sat there, when I put him to the breast, to show you how fine he was – your own first, fine son. You sat there, cracking your knuckles, and I looked up, and your eyes were murderous. You wanted to pluck him off me and dash his head against the wall. You said it yourself. You said it yourself!

ARTHUR

I was jealous. You know that. You forgave me. You said it was all right.

GUINEVERE

You are a barbarian.

ARTHUR

Oh, don't go on. That bloody look on your face reminds me of your family.

GUINEVERE

My family? Why blame them? You never see them!

ARTHUR

Oh, I see them all right ... in you!

GUINEVERE

It's more than I do. I'm in exile! You're surrounded with your own kin, even your bastards. This is your home, not mine.

ARTHUR

Not yours? How can you say that, not yours? Everything that's done here is for you. I work, I try to please – what more do you want, you've got a life! The trouble is – the real trouble is that I've always loved you more than you loved me.

She groans.

ARTHUR

It's true.

GUINEVERE

But I told you, at the beginning ...

ACT TWO

ARTHUR

Oh, I know you asked me to give you time, you messed me about a lot. It was considered a young girl's privilege in those days. *Were* you in love with me?

She shrugs.

ARTHUR

You seemed to like me.

GUINEVERE

I liked being made a fuss of.

ARTHUR

Well I loved you!

GUINEVERE

You desired me!

ARTHUR

If you weren't sure, then why did you marry me?

GUINEVERE

In the first place, you warned everyone else off. You put your hand on my arm in public. You used a special voice when you spoke to me. You were a king! People started talking to me who'd never even acknowledged me before ... asking me for favours ... treating me like some sort of public event, which of course I was. It all went to my head. I was only a second daughter. That yellow dress belonged to my sister. They weren't expecting you to look at me.

ARTHUR

Are you telling me, after all this time, you were talked into it?

GUINEVERE

GUINEVERE

I didn't say that. *(Irritable.)* Stupid bashed face, sitting there, talking to my brothers ... You wouldn't go away!

ARTHUR

You didn't seem to mind.

GUINEVERE

I was frightened of you!

ARTHUR

Why?

GUINEVERE

Because I knew you wanted to do something to me. But ... they showed me the wedding dress ... Let me wear the poplar leaves with the pearls.

ARTHUR

They were my pearls.

GUINEVERE

They were only river pearls. They were very milky. Still, it gave me something to play with while that old fool was yabbering over us.

ARTHUR

You mean the marriage ceremony? Didn't you take it seriously?

GUINEVERE

You were looking cow-eyed and stupid enough for both of us.

ARTHUR

You thought our wedding a joke?

ACT TWO

GUINEVERE

Of course. Didn't you?

ARTHUR

But you made vows! To love ... honour ... obey! You were given by your father until death do us part!

GUINEVERE

And you believed all that?

ARTHUR

They were vows!

GUINEVERE

Oh ... I don't remember much about it.

ARTHUR

Well try. It's important.

GUINEVERE

I've forgotten.

ARTHUR

Think, woman!

GUINEVERE

I can't.

ARTHUR

What do you mean, you can't? Can't you think?

GUINEVERE

No, I can't. Thoughts come to me. That's different.

ARTHUR

(Mutters irritably, then:)

So, you took it all as a joke?

GUINEVERE

Some virgin fellow, mumbling over us?

ARTHUR

What did you think the ceremony was for? To pass the time of day?

GUINEVERE

Oh, I knew what it was for all right. A property deal – between you and my father. And a licence to copulate; to provide you with an heir for your spoils. Listen, I'd dangled my legs in church long enough to know that men in womans' skirts were rogues or fools and, in either case, certainly not on my side. What can priests know? They spit on their own flesh! Whoever the Deity is, she must be very annoyed.

ARTHUR

(Shocked at last.)

Hah! Hah!

GUINEVERE

I went along with it, of course. Priests can get vicious.

ARTHUR

I can see how your ideas suit your purpose. I can see that. So, you took the vows, as a young girl ... knowing, knowing that you were lying ... deliberately lying ... to me ... to your family and the Church.

GUINEVERE

Not necessarily. What I vowed might have come true. I couldn't tell, any more than you could. Any more than they could. There was no-one who could command us to love each other for the rest of our natural lives ... not even the gods themselves.

ACT TWO

ARTHUR

The gods? *(Pause.)* Ye-es. I've always known you were pagan. Couldn't put my finger on it, but there's always been that uncertainty ... that look in your eye. So how long did it last, your love for me? Or did it ever begin?

GUINEVERE

You were my husband.

ARTHUR

You never loved me.

GUINEVERE

That's not true, we've had some fine nights together. I don't mean when you're drunk.

ARTHUR

I have to get drunk sometimes. Sometimes I have to get drunk in order to ...

GUINEVERE

Why, are you afraid of me?

ARTHUR

Oh yes. I don't know why ... you've been my dog often enough. Still, I've always felt ... I've never ... there's always been ... What I really can't stand is that look on your face. Critical. Unadmiring. I can't take that.

GUINEVERE

It's all in your mind. My back aches. I get tired.

ARTHUR

I know that. I understand. And the children ... You've never had a lot of energy.

GUINEVERE

No ... well ...

ARTHUR

I realise we haven't all that much in common – never have had. Still, I have tried to ... In fact, I thought things were better between us recently. I've tried to ... come your way more. I've even tried to introduce a few ... cultural touches.

GUINEVERE

You mean, the pipers in the courtyard?

ARTHUR

I thought it might clear the air a bit.

She grins.

ARTHUR

I did it for you. I thought you'd be pleased.

GUINEVERE

It didn't occur to you to consult me.

ARTHUR

I wanted it to be a surprise.

GUINEVERE

It was a surprise all right! You don't know the first thing about music.

ARTHUR

Well, I don't have the time.

GUINEVERE

Oh God.

ARTHUR

I thought it would please you, that's all.

ACT TWO

GUINEVERE

You mean they saw you coming.

ARTHUR

All right, all right. You're the one who knows how to spend. You're the expert in that quarter, I freely admit.

GUINEVERE

Oh, I'm allowed to shop. That's what shops are for, isn't it? Can't have a kingdom without shops. The whole nation would fall about our ears in a fine mist!

ARTHUR

What's wrong with trade? Very good thing in its place.

GUINEVERE

I agree. No substitute for the sword, of course – for the clean spilling of blood. But, for females, and the obese, the crippled, and the eunuchs ...

ARTHUR

On the contrary, I see a great future for the market. The law of contract is a fraternal notion. You've backed me there.

GUINEVERE

And the Grail?

Pause.

ARTHUR

What?

GUINEVERE

The Grail. The Quest. For the highest, the rarest, the purest. As you put it. Where does that fit into your market economy?

They lock stares. He breaks away.

ARTHUR

Leave it.

She makes to speak, but he goes on.

ARTHUR

Peace and equality aren't bad aims. Oh, you can sneer if you like. I've been reading about the Phoenicians. Clever buggers, the Phoenicians. They stay out of trouble and supply both sides. Neutrality's the game. We must build more ships.

GUINEVERE

Not by cutting down my oak forests, you won't! You cut down one more tree and I'll put a blight on you that will shrivel your balls to peanuts! Do you really think you'll get the English – those mysterious people – to rise to the rallying cry of *Deficit!*?

ARTHUR

We've achieved substantial improvements in living standards.

GUINEVERE

But the cost! We're stifling ... deafened ... drowning in maintenance and floating in debris.

ARTHUR

We can recycle.

ACT TWO

GUINEVERE

And who's we? Not you and your bloody knights ... too busy down at the club cashing up new schemes to add to the detritus.

ARTHUR

Oh, come on, you've sat on the boards yourself ... you're eloquent enough when it comes to babies. I know it's not romantic enough for you, but who feels the cold, you or me?

GUINEVERE

I'll stoke my own fires rather than condemn other women's sons to monotony. Making them choose one craft ... for a lifetime ... what sort of existence is that?

ARTHUR

It's rhyme and reason.

GUINEVERE

They'll never stand for it.

Slight pause.

ARTHUR

(Mutters)

I tried the other way and it didn't work.

GUINEVERE

What?

ARTHUR

I tried the other way ... listening to you. A mistake. So, lonely, I've been more materialistic. It's what people want. They want things. They want their share and they won't be satisfied until they get it. And it's no good telling them that the bosses don't

change because their titles change. Change they want
and change they'll get because people ... people ...

GUINEVERE

Get bored.

ARTHUR

Aye. It's a wasteful process, the pendulum ... an
innate sense of husbandry against a rage for justice.
And I'm tired. I can't fight everybody.

GUINEVERE

You've zonked a few in your time. We couldn't have
done it without you.

Pause.

ARTHUR

I can't kill you. I should have no-one to talk to.
(Pause.) Give him up. Please.

GUINEVERE

(Whispers)

Don't.

ARTHUR

Please. For my sake.

GUINEVERE

No. I can't.

ARTHUR

You bitch. You slut. I'd like to slice you up and hang
you on a hook.

GUINEVERE

Don't.

She caresses him. He breaks away, then begins to knock her about.

ACT TWO

ARTHUR

Love me. Love me, dammit! Love me, do you hear me? Love me!

She escapes from him.

ARTHUR

What can I do?

GUINEVERE

Don't do anything!

ARTHUR

I want to kill you!

She approaches him, climbs on to his lap. They make love.

GUINEVERE

Cave ... abyss ... full sea ... don't be afraid ... listen, can you hear the bell under the waves? Bowels full of wet mushrooms ... plunge into the forest ... through the thicket ... spikes ... wet grass ... oh, the moss is wet and shining but will it hold? Can you hear her, the princess?

ARTHUR

It's dark.

GUINEVERE

Don't be afraid. And don't hold on so tight. Breathe. Deep. Down through the swell, green bubbles, seafields ... cut the turf, part the weed ... and die, die, die.

Pause.

GUINEVERE

GUINEVERE

A man is ash. *(She wipes his forehead, and whispers.)* The weakness is temporary.

Light change.

GUINEVERE sits at his feet, holding his knee.

GUINEVERE

But what did you want? What did you expect from me?

ARTHUR

Love. And fidelity.

GUINEVERE

At least I care enough to deceive you.

ARTHUR

Oh yes. Deceit. We know all about that. We know about deceit all right.

GUINEVERE

Do you think I wouldn't have been faithful to you if it were humanly possible? Of course, I would. I like you.

ARTHUR

Not enough, it seems.

GUINEVERE

Look how well we've been getting along lately. It's been better than ever. Let me deceive you. You'll be happy.

Light change.

GUINEVERE

You take me to feel strong. No matter that you always feel weak and unhappy after. You lay waste to me and complain that it makes you unhappy.

ACT TWO

ARTHUR

A man always feels like that after a woman.

GUINEVERE

Why? Why?

ARTHUR

How should I know?

He gets up, and does up his trousers.

ARTHUR

What the hell am I going to do? What am I going to do? Tell me. They'll all know ... *(He indicates outside)* ... you've been getting round me. What am I going to do?

Pause.

GUINEVERE

I want a seat on the council – with an equal number of elected women.

ARTHUR

Women? Women in council?

GUINEVERE

Yes, women. Chicken-boned, pea-brained, moody, hysterical women.

ARTHUR

(Restraining his mirth.)

It's been tried. Before your time. Oh, a few came forward. Nothing special ... a few grannies in the Ministry of Health. Nothing ... radical.

GUINEVERE

First steps! Not that they weren't brave women, to endure your barracking. But they were so gratified to join that they played it your way. Neat suits, dry manner, and no bulges visible. But we do bulge. Half the world bulges! And we've learnt from you. From your mistakes. I've no intention of being tried by all those men. I want my women on the council. Then we'll see.

ARTHUR

Bollocks.

GUINEVERE

There's something you ought to know.

ARTHUR

Yes, I gather you've been spending time with Merlin. *(He shifts, uneasily.)* Some ... brew? Some new formula? What's he doing? Breeding women with two cunts?

GUINEVERE

Something like that. *(Idly.)* Cloning.

ARTHUR

Cleaning what?

GUINEVERE

I didn't say cleaning! Clone. To clone. Cloning.

ARTHUR

And what's that supposed to mean? I can tell you now there'll be no budget for it, we're overspent as it is.

GUINEVERE

We don't need you, we don't need you, we don't need you! We can breed ourselves. Women breeding women. Not men. Not men. Men aren't needed. We can breed women on our own. What do you think of that? What do you think of that, trying to kill me off! You

ACT TWO

can't do without us, but we can do without you! We
can make as many Guineveres as we like. A hundred!
A hundred thousand Guineveres!

ARTHUR

Good Christ.

GUINEVERE

Guinevere ... Guinevere ... Guinevere ...
Guinevere ... Guinevere!

ARTHUR

Bloody nonsense.

GUINEVERE

Ask Merlin if you don't believe me. He's outside.

ARTHUR

Cloning! You'll have to do better than that. You know,
you're a disappointment. I expected something more
subtle. For Christ's sake, woman, you're on trial
for your life. Will you please state your case! Five
hours in the council chamber – during which you
sulk, waste the time of the court with irrelevant
depositions, and set about your own lawyer! Seven
hours yesterday trying to find a way to save your
neck without destroying me, the kingdom and
everything that's been built in the last twenty years.
And you? Fresh as a daisy! Lively, garrulous and,
yet again, completely off the point! Will you get the
message? They want you dead. They want you under
the ground!

Pause.

GUINEVERE

And will you let them? Put me under the ground?

GUINEVERE

ARTHUR

I've a right to demand it. There's hardly a knight who hasn't been mentioned by name.

GUINEVERE

Two were a bit young. One was frightened – he couldn't manage anything. And the Chevalier ... he likes fat women.

ARTHUR

So, it's really true?

GUINEVERE

Oh yes. I've been generous.

ARTHUR

(Sneers.)

Noblesse oblige? A sort of royal largesse?

GUINEVERE

No. No. Patronage. I've suited myself.

ARTHUR

(Baffled)

What then?

She does not reply.

ARTHUR

He was my best friend.

GUINEVERE

What difference does that make?

ARTHUR

Does that not mean *anything* to you?

ACT TWO

GUINEVERE

Your best friend. My lover ... your best friend. My lover. *(Slight pause.)* You have women – I ... have men.

ARTHUR gazes at her, frowning, and then sees daylight.

ARTHUR

Ah! Aha! I see! Spite! You did it to spite me. You've been doing it to pay me back! Oh my God, how I must have damaged you to make you ... And I'd no idea, no idea at all. *(He approaches her soberly, and takes her hand.)* I'd no idea. Yes, I can see ... see the nest of worms. I've been ... It's true. I've neglected you. I haven't always come straight back. There have been lies. They were to protect you. But yes, I have lied. I've deceived you. I've damaged the thing nearest to my own heart, my own dear wife. Seeking for truth out there – the highest, the purest ... I've ... I've ... and you've punished me where it was bound to hurt me most. Put a knife in my heart! Of course, it had to be my best friend, I see that now. My God. Oh my God! How I must have hurt you that you should ...

GUINEVERE

(A screech.)

How many more times must I tell you! It's nothing to do with you! It's not your affair – any of it!

ARTHUR

(Shouting.)

Don't shout!

She tries to pull away from him.

GUINEVERE

ARTHUR

Let's try to keep it private.

GUINEVERE

He has dark blue eyes and he has only to look at me. It has nothing to do with you. Leave us alone.

ARTHUR

All right, don't shout. I'm trying to understand. Can't you see, I'm trying to understand! *(Pause.)* Yes, so ... It's an overwhelming, mutual ... *(Grinds out the word)* ... passion.

He turns on her glaring and ferocious.

ARTHUR

You lying bitch. You're a lying bitch! What about all the others. Gawain, Peredur ... even Mordred. My God – tainted from the first ford. From the first swing into the saddle. And we dragged ... *(He laughs, bitter)* ... dragged equipment over mountain passes ... all that mud ... a forest of thorn that took us a summer to cross. That bloody summer with the flies feeding on our sores. And it was here ... here. Find the Grail! When our calf muscles trembled, when we retched bile ... sweated with fever until our eyes stood out of our heads like eggs, we whispered, through cracked black lips ... the Grail! Oh God. The hobbles were on before we left the stable yard. All our manhood, and I don't even know if my sons are my own.

GUINEVERE

The first one's yours if you're worried about inheritance. He's not the brightest.

ACT TWO

ARTHUR

And my girls ... my little girls ...

He attacks her.

ARTHUR

I want to know. All of it!

GUINEVERE

(She struggles.)

Stop it.

ARTHUR

All of it!

He shakes her by the neck, and spits full in her face.

GUINEVERE

Take your hands off my neck!

ARTHUR

Whore!

GUINEVERE

(She can hardly speak.)

Stop it!

ARTHUR

No wonder you could teach me tricks.

They struggle. She manages to free herself.

GUINEVERE

(Baleful with fright – cornered.)

Somebody had to ... You weren't fit to let loose as you were.

He makes to strangle her. She gurgles, a horrible sound.

He drops his hands, shocked. She staggers away from him, gasping and gasping for breath. She recovers, feeling her neck painfully, moving well away from him.

ARTHUR

Kill her. Why don't you kill her! Like a gnat against a wall? Find myself a fresh young girl. Breed a new family. At least they wouldn't have that bloody quick look on their faces.

GUINEVERE

Oh, don't say that about your own children. They're sharp enough to survive. You should be grateful for that.

ARTHUR

Well, nothing's ever right for you. I conquer a country, return home in triumph. Do you laugh, do you greet me? No! You complain of my being away. But when I'm home, if I stay too long, you complain again. I bring mud in. The yard is full of machinery. There's hawkshit in the airing cupboard. I buy you jewels. You leave them on the sink and say that anyway, what you really want are shells! So, I lose two men's lives bringing you shells from Scythia and what do you do? Give them to the cowman!

GUINEVERE
(Sullen)

They weren't the right ones.

ARTHUR

They never are. Nothing's ever right.

ACT TWO

GUINEVERE

How can it be? How can it be? When the sum of your whole life is sitting in a tower listening to birdsong. Drying your hair by an open window for freedom – how can it be? You couldn't begin to fill my dreams. Who could? You come back, sweating. Scarred. And we bathe you and feed you. And you feel wonderful. We can feel how you feel, and it must be wonderful! You expect to find us full of energy, but we're limp. We, who have been doing nothing! But you forgive us. We're only women, after all. And you tell us stories. And we listen. And *what's the use?* What's the use of that?

ARTHUR

Guin...

GUINEVERE

It's not that we think we'd do better than you. We're not romantics – God, we bleed every month. But we do have arms and legs, even if they are weaker than yours ... and we do have minds – ingenuity. Must it forever rot within us, the fruits of our experience? What's right is what you do yourself! You settle for less than perfect then – no need for visions, fantasies ... the consolation of the pillow. Of course it never suits! To be told the story is *not to do it!* To be told of your lives is not to live it. You *have* your life.

ARTHUR

Nonsense.

GUINEVERE

All I've ever needed was a good bay thoroughbred.

GUINEVERE

ARTHUR

Rubbish! You'd be prey to the first brigand on a narrow path! Who'd stop the Hun from slicing the baby out of your belly? Oh, you're glad enough of my strong arm when we're under attack, well, my prick goes with it, so let's have less of this new regiment of women of yours. Do without us? You must be forever creating us, and we're never right. We never do. We're your work! Try making a better job of it. You haven't made Gods of us so far ... nor of yourselves. A place in council? Why should we let you in? What have you got to offer? Except your moods.

GUINEVERE

I knew Mordred was plotting against you a full year before you would even listen to me.

ARTHUR

Yes, and what about all the other times you woke me up? The dreams that were false? If instinct's so bloody marvellous, why haven't you put it to work? Listen, who invented the wheel? A woman? While you lot sit in the orchard with your bellies up sewing buttons on your hems and whining about slavery, some poor sod ... a man, of course, is breaking stones for your rockery.

GUINEVERE

I don't wear buttons on my hems. What are you talking about?

ARTHUR

Oh God! *(Pause.)* Look. If I let you in, will you stop all this?

ACT TWO

GUINEVERE

What do you mean?

ARTHUR

(Grinds)

Stop seeing him.

GUINEVERE

(Slight pause.)

You mean you'll trade?

ARTHUR

Nothing wrong with that.

GUINEVERE

Compromise is all?

ARTHUR

Yes. The other's too easy. You haven't answered my question.

She does not reply.

ARTHUR

Can't you see your way? For me? For the children?

She groans.

ARTHUR

Please Guin.

GUINEVERE

Stop it.

ARTHUR

I can swing it in there. I've got a few things up my sleeve. Don't think I don't know what's going on. It's political. They're trying to split us. Use us against each other. All we have to do is stick together. We've

been there before. We're old hands, you and I. All I
need is your word.

GUINEVERE

(Low)

If I gave it, I couldn't keep it.

ARTHUR

Please.

GUINEVERE

There's no point in your asking.

ARTHUR

Is it mental, or physical, or what? I'll help. How can I help?

GUINEVERE

By keeping out of it!

ARTHUR

No, no, I can't do that. I love you.

GUINEVERE

What's that got to do with it?

ARTHUR

I can't get to you! God dammit, I hate it when you're like this. You go away from me. Guin, for pity's sake!

GUINEVERE

Get your hand off my ankle! It's been the same from the beginning.

ARTHUR

But I love you!

GUINEVERE

That's your affair! Keep it to yourself!

ACT TWO

ARTHUR

You run away all the time!

GUINEVERE

In God's name, what else can I do?

ARTHUR

I can't stand it when you're like this. When you're unkind to me, I ... I ... It's the same when we're apart. You know ... I get restless. Then the off. I can't wait to get away. Well, yes, even from the sound of your voice when things are stale between us. It's true. It's true. I chase everything. You've always known that. You've always been ... I've loved you for that. But I don't know ... after a few weeks, the energy goes. I seem to lose definition without you. I lose my shape.

GUINEVERE

Please stop.

ARTHUR

I'm just trying to make you understand what you mean to me ... How much I need you.

GUINEVERE

You put me in prison, and then you want consolation for your freedom. If you loved me. That is, if men could really love. Love. Then you would let me go. You would take the risk. You would set me free.

ARTHUR

You? Not free? But of course you're free! Arthur's queen not free? My whole life has been about freedom. Full representation for the Welsh ... The marsh tribes ... Freemen's rights ... guild right ... serf's rights. You not free?

GUINEVERE

GUINEVERE lifts her head in soundless laughter, and moves her arms, as if inadvertently exposing the thong marks on her wrists.

ARTHUR

Oh, yes, well ... I know that you have ... you have suffered. But if we finish this business sensibly, like adults. I shall see to it that the areas of your involvement are immediately enlarged. You and your women, will be allowed – no, requested ... asked to contribute more fully. Fully to our social and civic. And, yes, and political life – without upsetting the children's routines of course, I know you wouldn't want that. No, no. I respect your stand. I comprehend. I perceive the nature of your restlessness. We men must enlarge our hearts. You are right to chide us. We have taken you for granted too long. Who knows what your contributions might be ... given your heads ... Might be very imaginative. Perceptive. Civilizing. No, I applaud your stand. Even against me, your husband, the king. I am proud of you. We'll give you some real power. Ha ha ha! Shock the life out of them. But ... no more time for fun and games. Have to keep your nose clean from now on. Particularly as a new girl.

He smiles at her waggishly.

GUINEVERE

Oh, you bastard, You bastard. You cunning, black-hearted, manipulating bastard. You will not move one inch, will you? Not one fraction of an inch. It must all be about you, to do with you, relate to you. Even the plots. Even the plots must be about you. If I fight, it must be you I fight. You will be the hero – the virtue attacked. By God, you will even be the villain

ACT TWO

rather than take one step out of the light! How often must I try to tell you? What must I do to make you understand? *It has nothing to do with you!* What means must I employ to nail it into your head? I consort with whom I please because that is what I am. He excites me! When he comes into a room, for me, the air changes. I love his knuckles, his wrists, the hair on his back. I suck the grit from his bent, black toes.

ARTHUR

(Groans)

Stop it.

GUINEVERE

I love his smell. The little blue cushion, with the embroidered cormorant, is stuffed with his hair. I've even collected his sick in a silver bowl.

He groans.

GUINEVERE

(Soft and secret)

I have a secret garden where I grow fruit for him. And iris root, for his body; marigolds for his bath, wild lupins for his floor.

ARTHUR

(Breaking down.)

But you don't weave linen for him.

GUINEVERE

No, I weave linen for you. For Lancelot, I weave silk. My cellars are full of it. Coffers of stained silk. Oh, don't cry! Don't cry. Please don't cry.

But he cries.

GUINEVERE

ARTHUR

Why?

GUINEVERE

Because he's beautiful. You know he is.

ARTHUR

But he doesn't love you.

GUINEVERE

What's that got to do with it? Who's talking about love? I love you. Except when you're drunk on the dance floor, showing me up and bawling in my ear.

ARTHUR

Then why can't you give him up? If he doesn't ... If you don't ... It isn't fair! I try so hard, all the time, to do my best to please you. To please the country. Your way isn't right. It's unreliable. Where's that going to get us? You're idle. Yet you're happy. I hear you laughing. Laughing, when I'm worried to death with affairs of state. It's so unfair!

GUINEVERE

You shouldn't have married the daughter of the Marsh King.

ARTHUR

Jumped up rag and bone man.

GUINEVERE

He knew how to survive.

ARTHUR

He'd be in the clink if he were alive now. We can't let everything run wild the way it used to.

ACT TWO

GUINEVERE

You have no more control over my body than I have myself. Take it up with God, not me. If you can't amuse my nipples, no law is going to do it for you.

ARTHUR

(Louche.)

I can turn you on.

GUINEVERE

Join the club.

ARTHUR

Whore! One minute you're talking sense. You're never in the same place two minutes running!

GUINEVERE

Is the weather?

ARTHUR

We have to put up with that.

GUINEVERE

You mean you can't beat it up, break its nose, bash its head against the wall? The answer's no. No, I will not give up my present nor my future lovers. No, I will not sit at table on your terms, neither will I fight with your weapons. I am not you, I am not like you, I will not listen to those evil-eyed bastards out there touching me up with their eyes ... You should kill them!

ARTHUR

I've done my best. I've tried. My attempts at reason, as I should have known, have been, yet again, wasted on you. I've offered you leniency, protection, forgiveness. I've even conceded a place in council.

You have no intention of making even the smallest
concession. I open a door to you. Wide open. But will
you step through? Have you any intention of joining?
The hell you have. You are recalcitrant, unrepentant
and obstructive. Your influence, from the beginning,
has been subversive. Subversive! You've poisoned
everything valuable in my life's work. The whole
endeavour has been eaten away from the inside. Not
by the monsters without – the twin dragons of St
Morgan, the seeping mere, the flesh-eating eagles –
the soldiers' shields crushing the life out of a man's
chest ... No. By you. The woman. The Mother. The
Queen! It is you. You who have contaminated the
Grail! My whole life ... all those men ... all for the
Grail – and you have destroyed it.

Silence. A long pause.

>GUINEVERE
>
>*(Tender)*

You fool.

>ARTHUR
>
>*(After a pause)*

And that's all you can find to say?

>GUINEVERE

Chasing around the world. Nothing wrong with that.
I'd have gone with you. But you went for the wrong
reason.

She crosses. Turns.

>GUINEVERE
>
>*(Gently)*

You fool. I am the Grail.

ACT TWO

He stares at her.

GUINEVERE

I ... I, Guinevere ... am the Grail.

ARTHUR

(Thick)

No. Be careful.

GUINEVERE

I, Guinevere, am the Grail.

ARTHUR

(Blinking.)

I don't believe it.

GUINEVERE

Yes, you do. *(Pause.)* You think you run away from me, but you run in circles.

ARTHUR

I don't know. I'm bloody tired. I know that.

He puts out a hand on her. Gently, she removes it.

GUINEVERE

I'm not your pillow, nonetheless. Though the mistake is easily made.

ARTHUR

But why didn't you say? If you knew, why didn't you tell me?

GUINEVERE

You wouldn't have believed me.

ARTHUR

That's true. *(Pause.)* So, in the end, here I am to stay. By the hearth. To be led by women.

GUINEVERE laughs.

ARTHUR

Yes, you'd like that, wouldn't you? See me led by the nose – bloody tamed.

GUINEVERE

No, no, no. That's no good.

ARTHUR
(Hopefully)

No?

GUINEVERE

We want bold boys, gentle fathers, and merry, unreliable lovers. And we want to be free. Like you.

ARTHUR

You are free! As free as I am!

GUINEVERE

No. No, we're not. We've worn our shackles so long you don't even see them. You write stories about us. But if we *are* the princesses – rescue us!

Slight pause.

ARTHUR

I don't know about that.

GUINEVERE

You think you stand to lose?

He shrugs.

GUINEVERE

What do you lose? Think. No more guard duty. No nagging. Come and go as you please. No sons to

ACT TWO

threaten you and turn you out of doors when the time comes ... A more casual affection.

ARTHUR

I wouldn't know where I stood.

GUINEVERE

Yes. Unpredictable. But exciting.

ARTHUR

You can have too much of that.

GUINEVERE

You're afraid to risk?

ARTHUR

What about inheritance?

GUINEVERE

Would it be so disastrous to share?

ARTHUR

You believe that?

GUINEVERE

There will have to be changes. If we come in, things can't be as they were. Devolve. Take the weight from your shoulders. I *can share* the responsibilities with you.

She looks up at him. He looks down at her, frowning, speculative.

ARTHUR

(Absently)

We've kept them waiting long enough.

GUINEVERE

There's no hurry.

GUINEVERE

ARTHUR

If you want a place in council, the first thing you'll have to learn is to keep appointments. On time!

GUINEVERE

Oh ... rules.

ARTHUR

Structure!

GUINEVERE

We'll see.

ARTHUR

Are you coming in?

Slight pause.

GUINEVERE

(Careful)

On what terms?

ARTHUR

(Careful)

Renegotiation.

Slight pause. GUINEVERE suddenly throws up her arms, ecstatic.

GUINEVERE

I want to live!

ARTHUR

You know, I'm not stopping you.

She gives him a firm stare, then passes before him. He puts out a hand, restraining her.

ARTHUR

I'm not stopping you.

She pulls away and goes out. He calls after her.

ACT TWO

ARTHUR

When you get out of the kitchen, don't complain of the heat, that's all.

He pauses for a second, thoughtful. Then follows her off.

Light change.

GUINEVERE enters in a magnificent cloak, followed by ARTHUR, likewise. He takes her hand and sweeps her round the stage, as if presenting her – at first defiantly, then with increasing confidence and dominance from both.

GUINEVERE moves forward, away from ARTHUR, presenting herself. ARTHUR is disconcerted at first, then, as it were backing her move, sends a raking glance hither and thither, as if searching for dissent. He approaches her. She turns. They regard each other levelly. He offers his arm, but she bows without taking it. They present themselves to the audience, separate, but side by side.

Fade to black.

THE END

ETHEL

A MUSICAL PLAY IN TWO ACTS

Based on a true story

For James Hogan

"We had Ethel Merman on the show and,
afterwards, nobody could hear for a week."

JERRY LEWIS.

ETHEL

CHARACTERS

ETHEL MERMAN
BEE MADSEN
DOLORES LEEB
ROSE ILENE ROONEY
SAL MCBRIDE
CONNIE VAN BUREN
(doubling as:) THE DUCHESS OF WINDSOR
JUNE HOFFMAN
(doubling as:) MARIA

GARY
(doubling as:) IRA GERSHWIN
NORMAN
(doubling as:) GORDON
GEORGE GERSHWIN
PETER HELGUSON
(doubling as:) THE PRODUCER
COLE PORTER
DUKE OF WINDSOR

SONGS

LET'S FACE THE MUSIC AND DANCE
Irving Berlin (Irving Berlin Music Company.)

THE FLOWER SONG
From George Bizet's Carmen.' Public Domain.

JOSHUA FIT THE BATTLE OF JERICHO
Wolf/Lars/Traditional (Sony/ATV Music Publishing.)

PUTTIN' ON THE RITZ
Irving Berlin/Frank Halferty (Kendor Music, Inc.)

TIME AFTER TIME
Sammy Cahn/Jule Styne (Sands Music Corp.)

HEY GOOD LOOKING
Hank Williams (Sony/ATV Publishing.)

I GET A KICK OUT OF YOU
Cole Porter (Warner/Chappell Music Inc.)

EV'RY TIME WE SAY GOODBYE
Cole Porter (Warner/Chappell Music Inc.)

DON'T GET AROUND MUCH ANYMORE
Bob Russell/Duke Ellington (Sony/ATV Publishing.)
IT HAD TO BE YOU
Gus Cahn/Isham Jones (EMI Music Publishing.)

BYE BYE BLACKBIRD
Mort Dixon/Ray Henderson (Old Clover Leaf Music/Ray Henderson Music Co. Inc.)

SONGS

ANYTHING GOES
Cole Porter (Warner/Chappell Music Inc./EMI Music Publishing.)

I GOT RHYTHM
George and Ira Gershwin (Warner/Chappell Music Inc.)

BUT NOT FOR ME
George and Ira Gershwin (Warner/Chappell Music Inc.)

EMBRACEABLE YOU
George and Ira Gershwin (Warner/Chappell Music Inc.)

DOING WHAT COMES NATURALLY
Irving Berlin (Irving Berlin Music Company.)

ANYTHING YOU CAN DO
Irving Berlin (Irving Berlin Music Company)

THERE'S NO BUSINESS LIKE SHOWBUSINESS
Irving Berlin (Irving Berlin Music Company.)

LET'S DO IT
Cole Porter (Warner/Chappell Music Inc.)

NIGHT AND DAY
Cole Porter (Warner/Chappell Music Inc.)
I'VE GOT YOU UNDER MY SKIN
Cole Porter (Warner/Chappell Music Inc.)

YOU'RE THE TOP
Cole Porter (Warner/Chappell Music Inc.)

ETHEL

ACT ONE

ACT ONE SCENE ONE

The salon in the penthouse suite of the Holiday Inn, New Haven, Connecticut. It is furnished stylishly with plenty of seating, including two comfortable sofas. There is a radio and a reel-to-reel tape-recorder. Through windows, upstage, we can see it is snowing.

The Overture

Excerpts from ETHEL MERMAN's early hits, interspersed with sound-bites from her notices.

> "Girl Crazy heralds the birth of a new blues singer ... Miss Ethel Merman."

> "Ethel Merman is no tear-stained, voice-cracking broad. She approaches sex in song with the cold fury of a philosopher."

> "Ethel Merman, aiming just above the entrails, knocks you out."

During the overture, GARY the WAITER enters with a heavily-laden drinks trolley. He sets up a drinks tray, polishes glasses, and places them on the tray.

MARIA the MAID enters with an ornate flower arrangement; sets it down reverently, then leaves and returns with an even more ambitious display. She jerks her head for GARY to move the drinks tray. He watches her, concedes her choice of placement, and then goes – pinching her ass.

MARIA rearranges cushions, is not satisfied, goes and returns with bigger and plumper cushions, which she disposes with abandon. She steps back, reviews her handiwork, then remembers she has forgotten something and dashes offstage.

BEE MADSEN – Ethel's best friend – enters. A comely woman, not short, an ex-dancer. She wears a voluminous mink coat, boots with heels, fur gloves, and a large picture hat of fluted felt, creamy yellow, with a red poppy over one ear. Her coat and hat are sprinkled with snowflakes. The effect is quite attractive.

As BEE makes to take off her coat, MARIA enters with an enormous flower arrangement (which entirely hides her), and collides with BEE, entangling her in the profuse flora.

There is some business as they sort themselves out.

> BEE

Jesus, Maria!

MARIA brandishes the display.

> MARIA

Pretty good, eh Miss Madsen?

> BEE
>
> *(Laughs)*

Nope.

> MARIA

You don't think Miss Merman'll go for …?

> BEE

Nope.

ACT ONE

BEE gestures with her thumb. MARIA giggles, and manhandles the hideous flowers off. BEE takes off her coat, and shakes it out carefully to remove the snow, then chucks it over a chair. She pours herself a drink.

BEE

(Calls)

Merm? *(There is no response. She raises her voice.)*
Merm? *(Louder still.)* Mermo?

Offstage, ETHEL replies with awesome volume. (NOTE: her voice is much louder than anyone else's.)

ETHEL

What?!!

ETHEL enters. Like BEE, she is fashionably dressed in the style of the early 1950's – tight-waisted suit with a full, long skirt (post-Dior), a ruffled blouse, a lot of clanking jewellery, and coloured, high-heeled shoes.

ETHEL

What is this? Some sort of morticians' reunion? *(She is brought up short by the sight of BEE's hat.)* Wha –?

BEE stands her ground. There is a stand-off. BEE thrusts a drink at ETHEL, who swallows it in one, and prowls, inspecting the hat.

BEE

Cool, huh?

ETHEL

Are you kidding?

BEE

I look like Myrna Loy.

ETHEL

You do not. For God's sake, Bee! A picture hat? In December?

BEE

Shelter from the storm. Besides, it frames the face.

ETHEL

So, you're a landscape. And since when have you been wearing yellow? What sort of colour is that?

BEE

The flattering kind.

ETHEL

Who says?

BEE

Emile.

ETHEL

Oh Lord. *(She shakes her head in pity.)* What do you do to him?

She inspects the hat again, unnerving BEE. A thought occurs to ETHEL, stopping her in her tracks.

ETHEL

You didn't buy that in his salon? *(She pronounces it 'salonne.')*

BEE

Sure, why not?

ETHEL

Sitting down? At one of those little fancy tables with the pimp mirrors?

ACT ONE

BEE

(Aggressive.)

Yeah!

ETHEL

Bee. Bee. Don't you know? Never – ever – buy a hat sitting down!

BEE

Why the hell not?

ETHEL

Because it'll look – well – I don't know – *(She has forgotten the reason.)* When you stand up it's ... It can ...

BEE sits and stands.

BEE

What's the difference?

ETHEL

(Shrugs.)

Has to be something.

BEE

Who says so?

ETHEL

Cole.

BEE

Mr Porter? *(Conceding.)* Oh well.

They settle with a drink.

ETHEL

Fan Club arrived?

ETHEL

BEE

Yup. Just made it. Snow's pretty heavy.

ETHEL goes to the window to inspect the state of the weather. She looks out, craning down to look at the street below.

ETHEL
(Soft)

Wow.

BEE joins her and they look up at the huge, gently drifting flakes of snow.

ETHEL

Look at the size of them snowflakes. You ever see snowflakes that big?

BEE

We could be in trouble.

ETHEL

Kinda nice though.

BEE looks, in enquiry.

ETHEL

The way they move. *(She sways gently.)* Rain'll come straight down your cleavage. Snow's different. More of a ... a beguine.

BEE

Change the tempo, kid. This keeps up, we'll be playing to chair-backs tomorrow.

ETHEL

No, we won't.

They watch the snow, mesmerised.

ACT ONE

BEE

(Sings softly)

There may be trouble ahead ...

Starting a capella, ETHEL takes up the song: LET'S FACE THE MUSIC AND DANCE. As the MUSIC comes in, ETHEL and BEE circle each other lazily, singing in duet, their tempo in time with the snowflakes. They bow briefly to each other as the song and dance ends.

ETHEL

Okay, kid. Rehearsal.

BEE

Yeah. Better get down there while we still can.

ETHEL

(Going)

Without skis!

ETHEL exits. BEE puts on her coat, finds her gloves and bag, and waits – looking at her watch.

ETHEL returns. She has a dark, wild mink coat over one arm and carries galoshes. BEE holds the coat while ETHEL puts on her galoshes and swathes her hair in a large, gauzy scarf. She puts out her arms for the coat; does it up lovingly; puts on her gloves, picks up her bag, and turns towards BEE. A stand-off over the hat. ETHEL'S face is adamant. So is BEE's.

BEE

Oh, for Pete's sake!

She rips off the hat and dashes it to the floor. They contemplate it. Then BEE stamps on it with both feet.

ETHEL

Yee-haw!

ETHEL

She watches as BEE takes a woollen scarf from her coat pocket, and ties it tight round her head so she looks like a European refugee peasant.

              ETHEL

O-Kay. Bring on the chorus!

Shrieking like twelve-year-olds, they leave in a hurry.

Blackout.

ACT ONE SCENE TWO

Onstage at the theatre.

ETHEL and BEE arrive – their coats over their shoulders, now they're in the warm. They are escorted by the PRODUCER, and NORMAN, the Stage Manager.

The PRODUCER monopolizes ETHEL, while MEMBERS of the ETHEL MERMAN FAN CLUB SINGERS (EMFCS) wait apart in an eager group. BEE and NORMAN manage to prise ETHEL away from the PRODUCER who leaves, waving his blessings and adoration. Enter GORDON, the pianist, who sits at the piano with a wave to ETHEL, who pulls a silly face at him.

              BEE

C'mon. The Emfucks await. The Emfucks. E-M-F-C-S.
The Ethel Merman Fan Club Singers.

              ETHEL

Since when?

              BEE

Since you got them into all this.

ACT ONE

ETHEL

(With feeling.)

The Emfucks, huh?

She turns with a dazzling smile to the group; makes to join them; changes her mind, and turns back to BEE.

ETHEL

The Emfucks? For Chrissakes, Bee, we're supposed to be respectable!

BEE

What do you want me to do?

ETHEL

Change the name!

BEE

What you want, the Fan Club Occasional Festival Facility – F.C.O.F.F?

ETHEL looks ready to attack her, but contents herself with a terrifying scowl, hands BEE her coat, gloves, scarf, bag and galoshes. She shakes herself, wiggles her hands to relax, and bears down on the Fan Club, who can hardly contain their excitement. She shakes them all by the hand.

ETHEL

(To SAL)

We met before, didn't we?

SAL is a rangy woman with a shrewd manner.

SAL

Great memory, Miss M.

ETHEL turns to a little woman.

ETHEL

Hi, Rosy.

ROSY (ROSE-ILENE) gives her a sideways glare. ETHEL kisses CONSTANCE on the cheek. CONSTANCE, an Upper-Eastside lady with an immaculate hair-do, is the National Chairwoman of the Ethel Merman Fan Club.

ETHEL

Connie, great to see you. All set?

CONSTANCE

Oh, yes indeed, Ethel.

DOLORES

We're ready, Miss M!

The others nod, crowding ETHEL.

ETHEL

(Backing off.)

Okeydokey. Take it away! Over to you, Norm.

She nods to NORMAN, the stage manager, who corrals the GIRLS into a group, and gives them advice and instructions. ETHEL moves over to BEE.

ETHEL

Remind me.

BEE

(Indicating discreetly)

The one with the big ass is June, good voice – head and chest – has a lot of kids so favours this charity. Connie, you know. Never did figure what she's doing in the Ethel Merman Fan Club. She likes opera.

ETHEL

So?

ACT ONE

ETHEL goes into a sustained passage from THE FLOWER SONG, disrupting NORMAN's notes and getting a round of applause from the fans. ETHEL smiles and waves.

ETHEL

Just testing. *(To BEE)* Connie's a friend of Cole's. *(Nods towards DOLORES, a mixed-race girl.)* Who's the Dorothy Lamour?

BEE

Dolores. Joined by mistake last Fall. Came to what she thought was a Peggy Lee night.

ETHEL

Girls' got taste.

BEE

Yeah. Good contralto too. Her husband's a Teamster – fixes transport for us on the road.

ETHEL

Great. Just make sure you mask her. I don't want her upstaging me.

BEE

That'll be the day.

Their attention turns to the tiny witch-like WOMAN standing slightly apart from the group.

BEE

That one we know.

BEE AND ETHEL

Rose-Ilene!

ETHEL

(Sings, low)
"If you knew Rosy, like I know Rosy ... "

ETHEL

BEE
"Oh, oh, oh what a gal..."

ETHEL
Don't worry about it. Has to be one crown of thorns in a production – *(Mutters)* usually the second lead. Who's the big gal? Says we've met.

BEE
Sarah McBride – Sal – mystery lady. Texan. Don't know a thing about her except she can sure sink the stingers.

ETHEL
Texan, huh? *(She nods, crosses to the group.)* Gather round, girls. As you know, our show here in New Haven is the preview for Boston. Boston's the biggie so wrap up warm and don't catch a cold. You might give it to me. *(Lifts a hand to quiet them.)* In Boston, we'll be staying at the Ritz.

Awed responses.

SAL
Won't that eat into our take?

ETHEL
No, Honey. All on the house. Fixed by the local fans. This charity's popular, maybe because Boston has the best doctors in the world and they understand what we're trying to do.

ROSE-ILENE
What are we trying to do?

ETHEL
Good works.

ACT ONE

BEE

With Miss M giving up her name – which is precious.

The GIRLS applaud.

ROSE-ILENE

So, what's the charity? *(She turns to DOLORES, who feigns innocence, then to JUNE, who looks awkward.)* What are we singing for? Nobody told me.

Silence.

JUNE

(Small voice.)

It's medical.

ROSE-ILENE

What kind of medical?

CONNIE

I don't think we need go into any details.

ROSE-ILENE

I need to know.

Slight pause.

DOLORES

(Clears her throat.)

It's for women.

ROSE-ILENE

Women's diseases? What kind of diseases? Not –?

JUNE

Oh no. Not that.

DOLORES

Not at all.

ETHEL

ETHEL

If you really need to know, Rosy ...

BEE

She doesn't.

ROSE-ILENE

If I'm giving my middle C – twice – I need to know.

BEE

You don't – believe me.

CONNIE

Look, shall we move on?

ROSE-ILENE

Is somebody going to come clean, or am I walking? I've given more than my fair share to this fan club. I'm a founder member from 1935! Where do you get off, all of you, paytronising me after years of loyalty to Big Voice here. I've never missed a show!

ETHEL

(Losing it.)

Okay. Okay. We're doing this gig for black women in Africa who are suffering with fistulas, OK?

ROSE-ILENE

Fistulas? What is that?

BEE

(Sing-song)

Told you. *(To ETHEL.)* Tell her.

ETHEL

Right. Sure. Where's Gordon?

She looks round to make sure that he has gone, and there are no men present.

ACT ONE

ETHEL

A fistula is when you've given birth and it's such a disaster that your bladder or your bowel – or both – are torn so badly that you can't pee or – ah, go to the bathroom. Everything just runs down your legs, which means you smell of the john all the time. Which doesn't make you Miss Popular.

CONNIE

What happens is these women are banished from their villages. Their children are taken from them and they're driven out into the jungle to live as outcasts.

ROSE-ILENE

How the hell did we get into all this?

ETHEL

Bee read an article on an airplane. About two young doctors ...

BEE

Husband and wife.

ETHEL

They volunteered for six months in Africa ...

BEE

Seven years later ...

ETHEL

... they're still there.

CONNIE

Healing women ...

JUNE

So's they can go back to their villages ...

ETHEL

DOLORES
... and be with their children again.

ETHEL
We're raising money for medical and surgical supplies ... and to build a new hospital.

JUNE
Tell her about the dresses, Miss M!

ETHEL
Oh, and the docs had a great idea! *(A murmur of agreement.)* Guess it could have been the lady doc, huh? *(Agreement.)* When the women are all done with their surgical repairs, so's they can function properly and not smell like army latrines ...

JUNE
The hospital ushers them into this special, nice room ...

DOLORES
... which is just brimming with rolls and rolls of beautiful coloured cloth ...

JUNE
Flower patterns, birds ...

DOLORES
... leaves – squirly designs – anything they want ...

JUNE
And the women can choose ...

DOLORES
Whichever's their favourite cloth for a dress to make them look good as well as feel good.

ACT ONE

JUNE

To make them happy.

ETHEL

(Slight pause.)

So how about it. Rosy?

CONNIE

Isn't it wonderful? A worthy cause? Women helping women.

Slight pause.

ROSE-ILENE

I don't get it. The Ethel Merman Fan Club has a lot of male members – do they know about this?

ETHEL

Rose-Ilene ... just save your voice and concentrate on Boston.

ROSE-ILENE

If we ever make it ...

The GROUP turns on her in protest.

ETHEL

We'll make it. OK, folks, let's get to it. Connie, did you agree on your number?

Laughter.

CONNIE

Finally – after suggestions from high opera to scat singing, whatever that might be.

DOLORES

We got there.

ETHEL

ETHEL

So, surprise me.

The GIRLS go straight into JOSHUA FIT THE BATTLE OF JERICHO – acapella. ETHEL stops them after the first four bars.

ETHEL

(Genuine.)

Girls, that's great! I'm impressed. Just watch your voices. Keep the lemon and honey close. It's a tough time of year – *(She turns and calls)* Gordon! *(She gives a piercing whistle.)*

GORDON

Heard you the first time, Miss M!

Laughter, as he hurtles on to the piano stool. ETHEL crosses, they have a brief conversation; then ETHEL comes down centre.

ETHEL

Okay. I go, spiel, spiel, spiel, spiel – then ...

She breaks into PUTTIN' ON THE RITZ.

Light Change.

ETHEL segues into TIME AFTER TIME. She crosses the stage, makes a costume change, and we are in the nightclub, El Morocco.

ACT ONE SCENE THREE

The El Morocco.

At the end of the TIME AFTER TIME, ETHEL joins the DUKE and DUCHESS of WINDSOR. The DUKE rises, kisses ETHEL and takes her stole. The DUCHESS hands ETHEL a drink.

ACT ONE

DUCHESS

Champagne on the rocks – in a long glass.

ETHEL

Duchess, gal – you got my number.

She takes the drink. Calls of "Encore." The DUKE and DUCHESS rise and clap. So, ETHEL rises too and performs a short YOU'RE THE TOP. She swirls, pearls flying, glass in hand.

Light Change.

ACT ONE SCENE FOUR

ETHEL collapses on the sofa in the HOLIDAY INN suite, losing her finery en route. On the sofa, she and BEE relax – reminiscing.

BEE

You swapped jokes with the Duchess? Not *your* kind of jokes?

ETHEL

Why not? What's wrong with earthy? Earthy's not dirty. Nah, I told her my favourite – well, to kick off with.

BEE

Not the chicken joke?

ETHEL

Yeah, you remember. Farmer hears hollering from the hen house, goes out with his gun, sez: "Who's there?"

BEE

And a voice says: *(Accent.)* "Ain't nobody here but us chickens!" Did she laugh?

ETHEL

She'd heard it before.

BEE

You didn't do the one about the Irishman?

ETHEL

Yup.

BEE

Ouch.

ETHEL

She loved it.

GARY knocks and enters.

ETHEL

Hi, Gary.

GARY

Hi, ladies. D'you hear the news?

He resupplies the drinks trolley and tray, adds cigarettes to the large plated cigarette box.

BEE

Harry Truman wears women's underwear?

ETHEL

No. What?

GARY is bending over the radio – finds a news station.

RADIO

... and will be closed down. A state of emergency has been announced for the whole of Connecticut and

ACT ONE

Rhode Island. All transport is at a standstill and
emergency services are being handed over to the
National Guard.

He switches off.

> BEE
>
> Jesus!
>
> GARY
>
> We're fine here. You ladies need anything?

BEE smiles, shakes her head. ETHEL crosses to the windows, looks down at the scene below. GARY goes, and BEE joins ETHEL at the window.

> BEE
>
> My God. Nothing left. No street, no sidewalk, no cars –
> not even bumps to show where the cars were. Hey,
> suppose there are people inside, buried alive? Hey,
> where's *my* car? Where the hell is it?
>
> ETHEL
>
> Sitting under four foot of snow, not getting stolen.
> Gee, don't you love it? There's a style about snow, like
> God had another thought after making rain – came
> up with a better idea. *(BEE looks at her.)* It's so – I
> don't know – quiet. So ... good-looking.
>
> BEE
>
> Ask it out on a date.

A knock.

> BEE
>
> *(Calls)*
>
> Come in!

Enter CONNIE.

ETHEL

CONNIE

Sorry to intrude.

ETHEL

What's up? Don't tell me Rose-Ilene's quitting.

CONNIE

(Smiles)

No. You heard the news.

ETHEL

About the emergency? *(Nods.)*

CONNIE

People are coming in off the street. We've been helping in the lobby. The hotel is being magnificent. Beds are made up everywhere. Nothing's too much trouble. We've given our rooms to some hospital patients who're stranded. We're going to sleep in the corridor.

ETHEL

Connie, there's no need for ...

CONNIE

It's fine ...

ETHEL

Forget it. Bee and I'll take the sofas and you girls can fight it out in the bedrooms.

ETHEL indicates the two bedrooms, which are part of their suite.

CONNIE

Oh Ethel, thank you! I'll tell them.

CONNIE makes to go, pauses.

ACT ONE

ETHEL

What?

CONNIE

Rose-Ilene. *(Shakes her head.)* I doubt she'll be willing to share a room.

BEE

Tell her to boil her head.

ETHEL and CONNIE look at each other, accepting defeat.

ETHEL

Give her my room. The bed's king-size. Who knows? She may never be seen again.

CONNIE

(Laughs)

Thanks.

CONNIE exits, and returns with ROSE-ILENE, JUNE, DOLORES, SAL and CONSTANCE.

CONNIE

(To ROSE-ILENE)

Miss Merman has offered you her room, Rose-Ilene.

ROSE-ILENE

I'm not sharing, even with her.

ETHEL

Nope, you're on your own, Rosy. Best room in the house.

CONNIE takes ROSE-ILENE off. They return at once.

CONNIE

She doesn't like it. It faces the wrong way.

319

ETHEL

BEE points to the other bedroom. CONNIE and ROSE-ILENE cross and exit. A pause. CONNIE returns.

CONNIE

She says it will do and where's the bathroom?

BEE rises, and exits to the second bedroom.

ETHEL

My bedroom could house a brigade of guards. What's more, there's a dressing room with a divan and a sofa!

SAL

Don't worry, Miss M...

GARY arrives with blankets, which are sorted and taken off. ETHEL nods to GARY, points to the GIRLS and then to her open mouth. He nods and goes. BEE returns from the bathroom with ROSE-ILENE, now in a robe, slippers and shower cap. The GIRLS return severally. BEE mixes drinks. ETHEL puts a folded blanket for herself and BEE by each sofa. DOLORES watches in admiration.

DOLORES

Hey, neat, Miss M!

ETHEL

I was a stenographer, kid. Teaches you precision.
(Looks around.) Well girls, I have to say – QED – quite easily done.

GARY wheels in a trolley laden with food.

JUNE

Oh, wow!

ETHEL

Gary, you are magical. Just follow the Yellow Brick Road, there's a Gary at the end of it.

ACT ONE

GARY

Anything for you, Miss M. I saw 'Annie Get Your Gun' twenty-two times!

ETHEL

And I never missed a performance.

CONNIE

(to GARY)

Thank you very much. I hope we're not depriving anyone.

GARY

The Holiday Inn can cope, ma'am. Chefs are down there baking bread, defrosting ribs, breaking out the ice cream. Exciting, huh?

He goes, with a wave.

CONNIE

What a very nice boy.

DOLORES

Dishy too.

Musical bridge (music from ANNIE GET YOUR GUN.)

Light Change.

ACT ONE SCENE FIVE

The group has now eaten and is sitting around, warm and full. JUNE looks out of the window.

JUNE

This is awesome. I never saw anything like it before. D'you get snow in Texas, Sal?

ETHEL

SAL

Nope.

DOLORES

(At the window)

We could be anywhere.

JUNE

Or nowhere.

ETHEL

You're right. Know what it feels like? Like being in the war again. Everything out of shape; all the signposts gone ...

DOLORES

... and your life changed – completely.

JUNE

Mine did, that's for sure.

Murmurs. BEE gives her a drink.

JUNE

(Takes a drink.)

Thanks, Bee.

ETHEL

Not good, eh?

JUNE

(Hesitates)

You could say so. Doug, my husband, was always crazy to fly. As soon as war was declared, he went to Canada – volunteered.

DOLORES

But didn't you have young children?

ACT ONE

JUNE

Yup. Holden was still in diapers.

BEE

What happened, did he – was he –?

JUNE

Reported missing in action over Germany in '41. Ed was Doug's navigator. He'd missed the flight with the flu. Later, he came out to see me, to bring Doug's ... The boys needed a father!

SAL

You mean ...

DOLORES

You married the guy? You did it for them?

JUNE

I did it for me.

ETHEL

You don't have to feel disloyal about it. Because you lost Doug doesn't mean you have to ...

JUNE

He came back. In '46. Ed and I had just had Faye, our daughter.

ETHEL

Jesus, kid.

JUNE

Doug'd had a terrible time in Germany. After two attempts to escape they ... *(She struggles.)* ... his body was ruined. *(Pause.)* Ed's parents came down from Canada ... they were frantic about losing their first grandchild. What could I do? I had to go where the need was greatest.

DOLORES

... and you loved Doug.

JUNE

No. I loved Ed. Always will. Doug's fine. Still has bad nights – but we do okay. Know when I first saw you live, Miss M? 'Something For the Boys' – Alvin Theatre, '43.

BEE

Hey, I danced that show.

DOLORES

You're kidding!

ETHEL sings a few bars of HEY, GOOD-LOOKING. Applause.

BEE whistles ... laughter.

DOLORES

What's your story, Bee?

BEE

Me, I'm just a gypsy – a dancer. Merm and I met – when was it, babe?

ETHEL

1934. 'Anything Goes.'

BEE

Music and lyrics by –

ETHEL

The one – the only –

ACT ONE

> GIRLS
> *(Severally)*

Cole Porter!

Applause. Then quiet.

> ETHEL

So?

> BEE

So what?

> ETHEL

Make with the life story!

Murmurs of agreement. The GIRLS love this intimacy with their idol.

> BEE
> *(Glowering at ETHEL.)*

Which one d'you want?

> ETHEL

Cleanse yourself, girl. You're among friends, snowed under – who knows? You may never see Pittsburgh again. *(To the others.)* She was indicted for murder.

Gasps of horror. JUNE gives a little scream.

> ETHEL

And harassment. Not only of a Senator but also his dentist.

> BEE

For fuck's sake!

> ETHEL

Language Miss Madsen, nee Mankiewicz.

BEE

And balls to you Miss Merman, nee Zimmerman.

ETHEL

(Sing-song)

Language!

CONNIE

Don't mind me. I was in the navy.

JUNE

What happened Bee?

SAL

What was the verdict?

ETHEL

Guilty as hell.

BEE

Oh, for Heaven's sakes! I was sentenced for running down the Senator's pet alligator.

ETHEL

Willfully and maliciously killing an innocent beast.

JUNE

How long were you ...

DOLORES

Did they ...

ETHEL

She had to make a printed and verbal apology – in person – and give a donation to endangered species.

BEE

Of which he shoulda been top of the list – the jerk.

Laughter.

ACT ONE

CONNIE

'Anything Goes.' What a show!

ETHEL

Changed my life. That's for sure.

She begins to sing, very softly: I GET A KICK OUT OF YOU.

Her mood is reminiscent, but gradually becomes forte. The GIRLS applaud.

JUNE

Miss M, you are truly the greatest.

DOLORES

You make it sound so easy.

CONNIE

Right down the centre of the song, yet nothing expected, everything fresh – how do you do it?

ETHEL

(Laughs.)

Cole says I sound like a band going by. *(To CONNIE)* So, how was the navy? Didja sail the Seven Seas?

CONNIE

Yeah, the Mediterranean, and then the Pacific. I met my husband on a supply ship. We were torpedoed. It brought us together.

ETHEL

Well it would.

CONNIE

(Laughs)

The trouble with being in a war, nothing's ever the same again. You're just left, if you're lucky enough to survive, with the rest of your life. John goes to the

ETHEL

bank; I take care of our daughters. I guess it's the adrenalin you miss.

ETHEL

Try show business!

CONNIE

Oh, I'm not that brave.

The lights go out.

CONNIE

Ohh!

SAL

Hey!

BEE

Hold on. Stay put everyone! *(She stumbles in the dark.)* Yup. Radio's dead.

DOLORES moves to the window.

DOLORES

Street lights are out.

ETHEL

Looks like the snow is winning.

SAL

The army'll fix things.

GARY enters, a large candelabrum in each hand. Cheers from the GIRLS.

ETHEL

Gary!

CONNIE

Saved!

ACT ONE

CONNIE

Oh, bravo.

GARY

The main grid's down, so they say. We do have our own generators but it'll take a little while.

ETHEL

Don't worry about us, kid.

GARY

Thanks, ladies – hold on ...

MARIA enters with more candlesticks. The GIRLS applaud. She curtsies. MARIA and GARY go. ETHEL holds out her glass.

BEE

Coming up.

She refills glasses for SAL and DOLORES.

DOLORES

Thanks! *(Lifts her glass.)* Here's to the war-time spirit. Well, we won!

Laughter. Everyone drinks.

BEE

Good war, Dolores?

DOLORES

Nope. Got hitched, unhitched, hitched, hitched ... and hitched again.

ETHEL

What?

DOLORES

Married an infantryman. He got killed before the ink was dry. Married a fancy-assed captain who got an

ETHEL

Italian kid pregnant after Anzio; said her family was going to kill him. Probably a big lie. Anyway, I went to Reno. Did some war work in Pensacola, married an English flyer – dead within seven months. Engine failure. Met a saxophone player in New York. I was doing a little singing ...

ETHEL

You didn't ...

BEE

No – you couldn't ...

ETHEL

(In horror.)

Not a saxophone player!

DOLORES

I know. The skunk. After that, I wed a straight guy with his own business. Got two kids now. Dog. Cabin on the lake. Little place on the Keys. Life is sweet.

BEE

Yuh?

DOLORES

Sure. Just ... I'd like to have stayed with the singing.

ETHEL

You gotta nice voice, Dolores. No, I mean it. You're musical. Not too many singers are.

DOLORES

Why, thank you, Miss M. I think about it but, you know – the family.

ETHEL

So what? Do both.

ACT ONE

Her voice is sharp. A hiatus.

BEE

(To cover)

How about you, Sal? Were you in the services?

SAL looks at her without answering.

BEE

I just get the feeling you ...

SAL

(Cuts her off.)

Not really, no.

ETHEL

What does that mean? What was your job?

SAL

Travelling.

ETHEL

Where?

SAL

Oh ... Washington – London – Madrid.

JUNE

Madrid? In Spain?

ETHEL

Spain was a neutral country, wasn't it?

SAL

Kind of.

BEE

What were you doing?

SAL

This and that.

ETHEL

An awkward silence.

CONNIE
(Filling the gap.)
Ethel, I heard you at the Stage Door Canteen in '43, just before I shipped out.

She pauses – shakes her head slightly.

ETHEL
What's the matter? They gave me the bird?

Laughter.

CONNIE
No, no, no. You were wonderful. It's just the songs ... They stayed in my mind.

ETHEL
Good.

CONNIE
I thought the brass would have insisted on upbeat. Rally the troops. You didn't do that.

ETHEL
Nope.

CONNIE
You weren't afraid to make the men feel blue.

ETHEL
Nope. Songs stay in the mind when they tell the truth. That's what a real song is for.

ETHEL rises, steps forward, and stands – thinking back, remembering.

ETHEL
I was pregnant. Bob was in the navy.

ACT ONE

Murmurs and nods of confirmation from her knowledgeable fans.

Pause. ETHEL steps centre stage. MUSIC.

ETHEL begins to sing, softly: EVERY TIME WE SAY GOODBYE.

Light Change.

ACT ONE SCENE SIX

The Stage Door Canteen – during World War II.

ETHEL, in uniform, sings, with full backing: DON'T GET AROUND MUCH ANYMORE, and IT HAD TO BE YOU. Loud applause. Cheers and whistles from the G I's.

ETHEL kisses her hands to the BOYS. Opens her arms to them, waves, and leaves the stage.

Fade to black.

END OF ACT ONE.

ACT TWO

ACT TWO SCENE ONE

The Penthouse Suite at the Holiday Inn. Next morning.

MARIA enters to take away the breakfast trolley as ETHEL appears in a robe and big hair curlers.

ETHEL
Hi, Maria.

MARIA
Morning, Miss Merman.

ETHEL
How's the weather?

MARIA
Sun's shining but it's still snowing. Pretty weird, huh?

ETHEL
The Lord sure is trying to tell us something. Uh, leave the trolley.

She points to BEE, still asleep on the sofa.

MARIA
Gee, sorry, Miss Merman. D'you need more coffee?

ETHEL
No, this is fine.

MARIA goes.

ETHEL
Hey buster, shake a leg. Chop chop. Rise and shine.

ACT TWO

BEE stirs.

BEE

Oh God.

She sits up and looks around.

BEE

What city are we ... Oh! *(It comes back to her.)* Where is everybody?

ETHEL

Breakfast. Rosy was down, crack of dawn, to be first at the buffet. Didn't want to miss the breaded shrimp. The phones are still out. Gary says they're being fixed. Anyway, the girls are walking, wading, or sledging over to the theatre to see what gives.

She pours coffee for BEE who accepts it, but spurns the offer of food with a shudder.

BEE

Think we're okay for tonight?

ETHEL

Of course, we are. Won't have the out-of-towners, but we need a run. The girls haven't done this kind of thing before.

BEE

Mmm. Think it was such a good idea to use 'em? I mean – I don't know.

ETHEL

Can it. That's last night's intake talking.

BEE

They're amateurs.

ETHEL

ETHEL

So was I, back in Astoria.

BEE

That was then, and this is New Haven.

ETHEL

I gotta get dressed.

She exits. BEE refills her coffee cup. The telephone rings.

ETHEL

(Offstage)

Hey, is that the phone?

BEE

(Calls)

Yes! *(Into phone)* Hullo – Hullo, yes? – Norman? Hullo, how are you? Are the girls with you? *(She listens.)* What? Why? Can he do that? Yeah but why does he –? No, she won't. Sure, I'll tell her but – let me speak to Connie. *(She waits.)* Connie? So Norman said. Neither do I. She's in the … I'll tell her – call you back. Maybe you should stay till I've … Yeah. Okay, we'll get back to you. No, she can't, Connie. She doesn't have another free day for eighteen months! *(She puts down the telephone.)* Jesus Christ.

She gets up, finds a cigarette, and glances out of the window. She crosses and looks out at the lazy snowflakes.

BEE

(To the snow)

Look, would you lay off? We're in enough trouble!

ETHEL is singing offstage. She enters, dressed, and hair fixed.

ACT TWO

ETHEL

(Finishes her brief song.)

Remember what George said?

BEE

"Ethel, promise me – never, ever have a voice lesson." Merm...

ETHEL

And Irving said...

BEE

"If you write lyrics for Ethel they'd better be good...

ETHEL

... because everybody's going to hear them!"

BEE

Merm, they're cancelling the show.

ETHEL

I was singing in Fort Worth once... *What?!!*

BEE

That was the phone call. Alexis Friel is nixing the show.

ETHEL

What are you talking about? He can't do that!

BEE

Yes, he can. He's the producer.

ETHEL

Get him on the line – now.

ETHEL

BEE

(Rings out. Holds.)

Hi, this is Bee Madsen for Miss Merman. Miss Merman would like a word with Mr. Friel, please. *(She holds.)* What? Well find him! *(She puts down the telephone.)* Probably throwing up in the men's room. Should we go round there, rally the troops?

ETHEL

Nope. Get him over here.

She walks up and down, muttering.

ETHEL

Who does he think he is? I have the orchestra, the backup girls arriving...

BEE

If they make it...

ETHEL

Of course they'll make it! The Fan Club made it! They've put a lot into this, those girls – left their families, their jobs, and they're goddamn amateurs – excuse my French. How are they supposed to understand the knife in the guts, bullet in the back of show business...?

The phone rings. BEE picks up.

BEE

Hullo? Norm? *(To ETHEL)* It's Norm – stage manager.

ETHEL

I don't want the monkey. I want the organ grinder!

ACT TWO

BEE

(Into the phone.)

Norm, would you tell Mr Friel that Miss Merman fully understands. *(She pushes ETHEL away.)* She'd appreciate a word just to thank him for his efforts on behalf of us all. *(ETHEL gets the message.)* Absolutely true, a snowstorm is an act of God. Who are we to –? I'll hold the line.

BEE and ETHEL wave thumbs at each other and wait.

BEE

Hullo – Hullo? – Mr Friel? I'll hand you over to Miss Merman. Miss Merman?

ETHEL

Thank you, Miss Madsen. Mr Friel – Adrian?

BEE

Alexis.

ETHEL

Alexis ... so sweet of you to call, I was just getting ready to come into rehearsal. How may we help? Misunderstanding? Oh, surely not. Your crew yesterday were most helpful; we're looking forward to tonight. – I'm sorry, I didn't hear you. There must be snow on the line. – What did you say, Adrian?

BEE

Alexis.

ETHEL

Alexis, Alexis – are you there? *(She listens at length.)* Listen to me you little whey-faced bristle-brush, she's telling me Norm says you say the show is cancelled. The show is NOT cancelled. Because I say so! ...

ETHEL

What? Because I am the show, and I say the show is not cancelled! I don't care if the crew is stranded – to hell with the snow – what's with the excuses? What orchestra? It's a five-piece ... So fix some local guys, now! Let's see some action. Listen. Listen to me: when Ethel Merman says she'll show, she shows. Never mind the lighting. Anyway, that's a lie. The electricity's back on ... Well, it is here at the Holiday Inn. It is not impossible! It is possible and it will happen. Put Norm on the line. – Hullo? – Hullo? *(She puts down the telephone.)* He cut me off!

BEE picks up the phone, dials.

BEE

Could I speak to the Stage Manager, please? *(She waits.)* Norm? The little prick put the phone down on Miss M. Is he there? *(Listens.)* So what? ... If he doesn't want to play we'll run tonight without him. He's only the producer. What do they do except get in the way? ... What do you mean, 'majority equity?' He holds the ground lease? Oh, give me a break. We'll get back to you.

She puts down the telephone. It rings at once. ETHEL paces.

BEE

Yeah? Norm? *(She listens.)* You're kidding! Yup – I'll tell her.

ETHEL

Tell me what?

BEE

Our distinguished producer has just quit the building and at this moment is being air-lifted out

ACT TWO

by helicopter along with two heart-lung machines,
a veteran with breathing problems and June Havoc
who has a 7pm curtain-up – what? *(She listens.)* Okay,
buddy, get back to you. *(Puts down the phone.)* It ain't
looking good. Their electrics are still out. There's
nobody in the building except Norm. He says there's
no heating, and no way we'll get an audience. The
radio's telling people to stay home. A man and his
German shepherd got suffocated by a fall of snow.

ETHEL

Jesus.

BEE

Snow one – people nil. Yup.

ETHEL paces, thinking.

ETHEL

We could try the university.

BEE

(Shakes her head.)

They'll be in the same situation.

ETHEL

We need the theatre. Try Norm again. Say we'll come
in and rehearse in our coats and mufflers – give him
time to fix up some kind of heating.

BEE

How? With what? Merm, the guy's on his own. How's
he supposed to ... Who'd handle ... I don't know.
Maybe we should ...?

ETHEL

No.

ETHEL

BEE

Mermy, we didn't make the snow. It's like Adrian, I mean, Alexis, said ... Act of God.

ETHEL

Yeah, yeah, well, if it was an act of God, it was for a reason. We just have to figure it out. *(She walks about.)* Maybe if we did the show at the theatre there'd be some kind of disaster?

BEE

Like Abe Lincoln being knocked off?

ETHEL

Could be. Or a fire. Or maybe the building collapses and people rush out and get crushed to death. Maybe we shouldn't play there.

BEE

Maybe Adrian's right.

ETHEL

Alexis. No, he's just a snurge. Right. Time for decision. We'll do the show right here in the hotel. Tonight. So's we'll be ready for Boston on Thursday.

BEE

Assuming we make it there.

ETHEL

Roads'll be clear in a couple of days. You're talking about the U.S. of A! Yeah! Perfect solution!

She whoops into THE FLOWER SONG in celebration.

BEE

Can it, Merman! Where we gonna play? In the lobby?

ACT TWO

ETHEL

No, stupid! The Function Room! It seats at least 500 people!

BEE

But what people? Who? Who's gonna come?

ETHEL

The guests! And all the other folks sheltering from the storm. It'll be like a gathering of unknown travellers drawn together by – by – by –

BEE

Snow!

ETHEL

– by Fate, dammit! Okay, we can't sell tickets but we'll get them to dig in their pockets. Anyway, we need the run. It'll still suit our purpose if nobody shows – well, apart from the timing. You need an audience for that.

BEE

Nice try, Merm, but it won't work.

ETHEL

Why not?

BEE

Because you don't have a lighting plot, a sound plot; you don't have decks, SMs, ASMs, doowah girls. You don't have a band! Musicians!

ETHEL

So, we do it acapella.

BEE

"We?"

ETHEL

ETHEL

You – me – and the Fan Club.

BEE

The Fan Club?! They're singing one number! Joshua!

ETHEL

Yeah, and they sound great.

BEE

Because they've been practicing for months! That's their repertoire – one number!

ETHEL

Bee, they're singers. Okay, amateurs, but they can sing. You helped audition them. Listen. *(She finds a tape in her bag.)* They've been getting together cross-country. They're keen!

There's a reel-to-reel tape-recorder on the dresser. ETHEL puts on the tape. The Fan Club sings in close harmony. BYE, BYE BLACKBIRD. ETHEL runs it for a few bars, then switches it off.

ETHEL

What do you think?

BEE

What else have they got?

ETHEL

(Reads from the tape cover.)

'Blue Ridge Round my Heart Virginia. *(BEE shakes her head. She's never heard of it, so ETHEL sings the first two lines.)* 'My Heart Belongs to Daddy' – 'Amazing Grace' – 'You Must Have Been a Beautiful Baby' – Schubert's 'Ave Maria.'

ACT TWO

BEE

Hah – covering the waterfront. *(She muses.)* I don't know, Merm ...

ETHEL

Come on ...

BEE

Who'll play piano?

ETHEL

Gordon!

BEE

If we can raise him. He's staying with some celebrity. Could be snowed in by now.

ETHEL

Connie plays piano.

BEE rises firmly at this.

BEE

I'll find Gordon. *(Pauses.)* Merm, the hotel'll never go for this. They've got their hands full.

ETHEL

They'll love it. Get the girls. I got things I gotta do.

ETHEL exits. BEE picks up the telephone, talks under bridging MUSIC, and then exits into the bedroom. She emerges at once in her mink coat, picks up her bag, notices her abandoned hat perched on a lamp, clamps it on her head defiantly, and exits.

Light Change.

ETHEL

ACT TWO SCENE TWO

MUSIC continues.

A KNOCK when the music ends. Another knock. CONNIE, JUNE and DOLORES enter.

> CONNIE
>
> *(Finding no-one there.)*

Oh.

> DOLORES

Miss Merman?

> JUNE
>
> *Hullo? (Calls louder.) Hullo?*

The telephone rings. CONNIE answers.

> CONNIE

Hullo. Bee! Where is everyone? Yes, we're – Oh. I'll tell Miss M, she isn't – yes, she is.

> ETHEL
>
> *(Strides in, ready for action.)*

Hi!

CONNIE hands her the telephone. She listens.

> ETHEL

Find him. Get Norm. Where's Norm? *(She waits, making reassuring gestures to the GIRLS.)* Norm? Norm, d'you wanna come over, manage the show for me tonight? Here – right here in the Holiday Inn, they're giving us all the support we need. *(Reactions from the GIRLS.)* My shy charm did it again. Norm, I need you, Okay? It'll be fine – trust me. *(Makes to put the phone down.)* And get Gordon. *(She puts down the*

ACT TWO

telephone.) Hi, girls! *(They greet her, dazed.)* Take a seat. Siddown, save your energy, you're gonna need it. Connie how good are your hands? *(She moves her fingers like a piano player.)*

CONNIE

I'm a modest player, Ethel.

ETHEL

Read music?

CONNIE

Oh yes.

ETHEL

Can you vamp?

CONNIE

Vamp?

ETHEL

Fill in – busk – cover the gaps, drown the disasters ...

CONNIE

I don't think so.

ETHEL

Because, if we don't raise Gordon and the Holiday Inn can't find us a piano player ... Enough people here, surely some of their mothers made them stick with the lessons. Don't worry, Connie, we won't use you 'less we have to. *(CONNIE sits abruptly, deeply alarmed.)* Now girls, where's Rose-Ilene?

DOLORES

Having her feet done.

ETHEL lifts her eyes to heaven and waves a hand, brushing this aside.

ETHEL

ETHEL
Okay. Now. We're doing the show here. Tonight. *(Quells their panic.)* We don't have a band; we don't have a crew. We may have a Stage Manager if Norm comes good. What am I talking about? He'll be here. He's a Pro. Anyway, be professional suicide to cross me – just kidding. Whaddya think? Great, huh?

CONNIE
Heavens. Well, you can depend on us. We'll give you all the support we can *(JUNE and DOLORES murmur fervently.)* How may we help?

ETHEL
Help? Babes – tonight you are the show. You will be sharing the list with me. You'll be doing the bridges, taking over the doo-wah – and – *(She brandishes their tape)* – performing a couple of your numbers that wowed me so much I was going to slot you in anyway.

The GIRLS are too stunned to speak.

CONNIE
Doo-wah? *(She is baffled.)*

ETHEL
Yup.

JUNE
What does that –?

DOLORES
Will we –?

ETHEL
Nothing to it. All you gotta do is listen – rehearse – and rehearse again till you get it

ACT TWO

right – without – without using up all your energy so there's none left for the show.

SAL enters, nods to ETHEL.

SAL

Seating's fixed. The head electrician will help out with a couple of spotlights – amplification could be better but the heating's working and there'll be a bar set up for the interval.

ETHEL

Fetch out the dinghies, girls.

DOLORES

Do you really, seriously think we can do this?

JUNE

My nerves will get the better of me. I know they will.

ETHEL

No, they won't.

JUNE

I'm willing, Miss M – honest – it's just that if I get rattled I tend to throw up.

ETHEL

Don't worry, June, all part of the profession. What do you think the fire buckets are for? I'll stick you on the end of the line. If you have to, you can make a run for it.

JUNE

Thank you, Miss M.

ETHEL

> CONNIE
> *(To Sal)*
>
> You don't happen to know if the hotel has a resident pianist, or if there's a pianist – any pianist – in the hotel?
>
> JUNE
>
> Who can vamp.
>
> SAL
>
> Sorry?
>
> CONNIE
>
> I'll sing my heart out tonight, I promise, but, oh dear, I have no faith at all in my capacity to do all the things you require. I'm afraid the naked truth is ... we don't have a pianist.

BEE appears at the door.

> BEE
>
> Dadah!

With a flourish, she produces GORDON.

> GORDON
>
> Hi, girls.

ACT TWO SCENE THREE

The Function Room at the Holiday Inn. A PIANO in situ.

The GIRLS, crowded together (Stage right) are in a bad state of nerves. Sounds of an audience on the P/A. The GIRLS peek out at the people.

ACT TWO

JUNE

So many people!

CONNIE

Where can they have all come from? I know the weather's eased ...

SAL

The hotel's crammed to bursting.

JUNE

Even so ...

DOLORES

They've come to see Miss M. *(Calls)* You can put another row of chairs along here, fellers!

Indicates just below the stage.

JUNE

No!

She looks down – miming reaction to this invasion – loses it, rushes offstage. BEE, glammed-up, joins the group.

BEE

Okay? Okay? *(They nod with weak smiles.)* Take it easy – no sweat, just leave it to Ethel. She'll do the spiel, fill in the gaps ... Oh, somebody said there's a celebrity in tonight, staying locally, how about that – I wonder who it is? Where's June? *(They indicate.)* Oh.

The audience sounds get louder.

GORDON arrives in a tuxedo and takes his place at the piano, with a smiling nod at the audience. The Manager of the Holiday Inn, PETER HEGULSON, also in a tuxedo, walks on to centre stage, and holds up his hand for quiet.

ETHEL

PETER HEGULSON

Ladies and gentleman ... Ladies and gentlemen ...
They say every cloud has a silver lining, and tonight
that silver-lining is here with us. Thanks to the
snowstorm – the beautiful snowstorm – we are able
to present you – our guests – and those to whom
we've been able to offer shelter ... *(Loud Applause.)*
Thank you, it's been a pleasure and I speak for all the
staff – I might add we're not alone – a lot of townsfolk
here tonight have welcomed people into their homes.
(Applause.) Folks – the rumours are true. Not only
is Miss Ethel Merman – the great, the one and only
Miss Merman – a guest of the Holiday Inn but, also,
she has agreed, together with the Ethel Merman Fan
Club Singers *(BEE, standing with the GIRLS, grins.)*
to perform the show that had to be cancelled at the
theatre. As some of you may know, Miss Merman was
appearing for the Fistula Charity – named to strike
a blow for mothers in Africa and to provide them
with sewing machines to make pretty dresses for
themselves and their children. Spreading happiness,
ladies and gents, never comes amiss. Miss Bee Madsen,
Miss Merman's assistant, is in charge of choosing
the fabrics for this worthy charity. *(To BEE)* We'll be
passing the hat round at the end of the concert. *(To
audience.)* I know you'll all be willing to show our
appreciation. Enough, folks. I'll get out of the way and
leave the stage for the inimitable, the dazzling, and
enchanting as ever Miss – Ethel – Merman!

ETHEL appears. Applause and cheers. She goes straight into
ANYTHING GOES fast and loud.

>Applause.

ACT TWO

ETHEL

And now may I introduce the Ethel Merman Fan Club Singers!

The GIRLS come forward. JUNE joining them at the rush, wincing under the bright lights. SAL lurks at the back. DOLORES, smiling, waves cheerfully; CONNIE takes a deep breath bravely.

ROSE-ILENE runs on in a pink and red sateen dress with paillettes, pushing herself into the centre. This gets a laugh but ROSE-ILENE's grim demeanor subdues the audience at once.

ETHEL

May I introduce Connie Van Buren, our
Chairwoman – Sara McBride from Texas *(Applause.)*
June Hoffman, all the way from San Diego *(Applause.)*
Dolores Leeb from New York City and Miz Rose-Ilene
Rooney from Minnesota! *(Applause.)*

The GIRLS, including BEE, step forward, arrange themselves, and sing: BYE, BYE, BLACKBIRD. Applause.

ETHEL steps forward. GORDON rises, brings her a high stool.

ETHEL sits, one foot hooked on a rung of the stool.

ETHEL

You know, I was just a nice, ordinary girl from Astoria, Queens, New York. Nothing great in the looks department, though I've never had any complaints about my legs. Only child, a little naive. When we moved to New York I thought you needed a passport. There was just this one thing: in the church choir, I sang louder than anybody else. It just came out that way. My parents, who are great, put me through commercial college, thanks Ma, thanks Pa. It's because I've been a secretary that I have a certain

ETHEL

poise. I can handle situations – like reading a contract. Comes in useful, believe me! I got a good job in New York with Mr Caleb Bragg of the B.K. Vacuum Booster Brake Company – I never did figure out what the heck we made – and I started to sing at night, working both sides of the street as they say. Lou Irwin heard me at the Russian Club, took me on and I started to do so well with supper work that I gave up the day job. I was happy – I was doing fine, just fine. Then, one day, Lou bells me – sez will I go along to this address on Riverside Drive where all the nobs live; and I ask why, and he says to meet Mr Gershwin and Mr Gershwin – Mr George Gershwin and Mr Ira Gershwin – who want to hear me sing. Can you imagine? George Gershwin! *The* George Gershwin – and his brother Ira who wrote all his lyrics! It was like being asked to meet God and his brother! *(She slides off he stool.)* I remember every bit of it to this day.

She moves up right, ditching her jewellery and changing her shoes.

Light change

ACT TWO SCENE FOUR

GEORGE GERSHWIN is seated at the piano, vamping idly, trying chords and runs. IRA, his brother, enters quietly, whispers in his ear. They both look up as the young ETHEL MERMAN arrives, clutching her handbag and her sheet music. GEORGE rises, speaks quietly. He is a shy man.

GEORGE

Miss Merman, good of you to call.

ACT TWO

ETHEL

Mr Gershwin, it's an honour. I'm ... I'm ... *(She loses it.)*

GEORGE

This is my brother Ira.

ETHEL

Please to meet you.

Ira shakes her hand.

IRA

Hullo. Miss Merman. Do you happen to read dots?

ETHEL

Oh yes, Mr Gershwin I sing in the Lutheran choir. I brought my music.

She proffers her sheet music but IRA hands her another sheet.

IRA

If you could – could you –?

GEORGE

Just – you know ...

IRA

Take a run at this?

ETHEL nods, and scans the score.

GEORGE

We're looking for someone to drop in a couple of little numbers ...

IRA

In our new show – Girl Crazy.

ETHEL nods, smiles nervously, and briefly looks at the score in her hand.

ETHEL

> GEORGE
> *(Quietly)*
> Miss Merman, if there's anything about the song you don't like, I'll be happy to change it.

> ETHEL
> *(Stammers)*
> No – no, thank you Mr Gershwin, this is just fine.

She gets the message, gives him the nod, and goes into I GOT RHYTHM – full pelt. GEORGE and IRA stare at her. She picks up her sheet music and bag from the floor by her feet.

> ETHEL
> *(To the audience.)*
> There was just this – silence. I thought: "Well, I did my best." Then –

> GEORGE
> *(From the shadows.)*
> There are several other songs we'd like you to sing, Miss Merman ... if you'd care to.

Light Change

ACT TWO SCENE FIVE

We are back in the present.

ETHEL comes downstage – the memory scene over – putting on her jewellery.

> ETHEL
> I thought I'd died. Gone to Heaven. *(She pauses.)* A couple of songs in Girl Crazy that you might remember.

ACT TWO

She sings BUT NOT FOR ME and segues into EMBRACEABLE YOU. The GIRLS sing JOSHUA FIT THE BATTLE OF JERICHO – ending with ROSE-ILENE's middle C. She steps forward to take a bow.

ROSE-ILENE

That middle C is in honour of Ethel Merman who stopped the show at the premier of *Girl Crazy* by holding the same note for sixteen bars – and had to reprise the whole number four times!

She steps back in grim triumph. ETHEL steps forward.

ETHEL

My very first fan. Thank you, Rose-Ilene. Life surely changed from that moment on. One day the subway and the five and dime, the next: white chiffon with a red cloche hat to set off the spit curls, two fox furs with dinky little faces, and brown and white spectator shoes. Couldn't believe any of it! The sables, the diamond pins, earrings, Chanel suits, and when I got the chauffeur and the car ... which I never used, it was quicker to walk! 1934. A show called 'Anything Goes.' *(Applause.)* Book by Wodehouse and Bolton, revised by Lindsay and Crouse, music and lyrics by Cole Porter – the one and only.

ETHEL

(Sings.)

I GET A KICK OUT OF YOU.

ETHEL

Thank you ... thank you. Let's cut to 1946. War over. Guys and gals home again. And to celebrate – a great new show!

Shouts of: "Annie! Annie Get Your Gun!"

ETHEL

Annie Get Your gun! Book by Herbert and Dorothy
Fields. Songs by – who else? Irving Berlin.

ETHEL, backed by the GIRLS, sings a medley of songs from 'Annie Get Your Gun.'

DOIN' WHAT COMES NATURALLY.

ANYTHING YOU CAN DO.

THERE'S NO BUSINESS LIKE SHOW BUSINESS!

Finishing strong, ETHEL throws up her legs on the stool, and laughs. Her attention is drawn to the wings. A MAN is sitting in a wheelchair, a rug over his knees. ETHEL runs over to him – bends, kisses him, has a brief conversation, then returns centre stage. She seems overwhelmed with feeling, but composes herself.

ETHEL

Ladies and gentlemen – ladies and gentlemen, I am
honored to tell you that we have a special guest here
tonight – thank you, snow – on account of he was on
his way to Boston to be at our charity performance.
ladies and gentlemen, I have the privilege to present
to you – Mr Cole Porter!

She breaks for a moment as Cole waves a gentle hand from the shadows.

ETHEL

As many of you will be aware, Cole had an accident
some years ago. His horse not only threw him but
rolled on him – breaking damn near every bone in his
body. He's had – I don't know – fifty operations on his
legs and he'll hate all this but what can you say about
a guy who goes on to write even greater music than
before. What can you say?

ACT TWO

Applause. She waits for silence.

ETHEL

To end our evening tonight, I would like to sing you some of the songs of Cole Porter. The incomparable Cole Porter – even if he has just told me my pearls are too long. You know it's funny – me, a broad from the sticks and Cole – well – Cole is a gentleman, born and bred. There's no way we could have a thing in common. And yet – we're friends. Perhaps it's because we are devoted to the same goddess, the goddess of Music. Perhaps because – I don't know – it's something to do with truth. We take each other as we find – there's such a wonderful trust in real friendship – apart from anything else you know you're not going to get away with anything. *(She takes off the pearls, tosses them away.)* Ladies and gentlemen – for your pleasure – and mine – some songs – the melodies – and lyrics – from the same hand – from the heart and soul of Mr Cole Porter.

ETHEL nods to GORDON, who plays an intro.

ETHEL sings the following:

LET'S DO IT.

NIGHT AND DAY.

I'VE GOT YOU UNDER MY SKIN.

She ends with YOU'RE THE TOP.

THE END

Also from Quota Books . . .

PAM GEMS
Plays One

THE INCORRUPTIBLE
GARIBALDI, SI!
THE TREAT

*

PAM GEMS
Plays Three

GO WEST YOUNG WOMAN
KING LUDWIG OF BAVARIA
NELSON
NOT JOAN THE MUSICAL

Q

AVAILABLE FROM: WWW.QUOTABOOKS.COM

MARS ATTACKS MEMOIRS
By Mila Pop

Reviews

A rare insight into the Tim Burton cult classic. Hear about Hollywood behind the scenes and the development of the Mars Attacks! movie. A must read for movie buffs and fans alike.

LUKE ETTENSPERGER

The Mini-Cooper of the literary world, this book is nippy and stylish, attentive to detail, with a disarming, quirky exterior that belies a deep intelligence and timeless design. Mila Pop is a great interviewer; her questions, as well as her delight at the responses Gems provides, show that she clearly loves the film. Jonathan Gems answers her questions generously and on many levels. He explains how the movie almost did not come about (the phrase 'madcap adventure' comes to mind) and offers funny and fascinating anecdotes about some of the people involved. He also gives us the inside skinny on how the film industry and Hollywood really work, and from there goes into how this paradigm can be seen throughout society. His great affection for Tim Burton and his girlfriend, Lisa-Marie, is very touching and transcends mere artistic collaboration. The book nails the sense of a collection of supremely talented people having a blast as they create unique and wonderful things – namely the movie itself, the friendships made along the way, and the interaction between Pop and Gems. It's an easy, happy read, over all too quickly. I look forward to more.

LEELA MILLER

A fantastic fun read. You will not be disappointed. It's like sitting on a couch with both Jonathan and Mila and hearing awesome stories on how a movie is written and put together.

PATRICK EVRARD.

I am so glad I bought this book 'cause I almost didn't after seeing the cover. Now I know the meaning of 'Never judge a book by its cover!' This is the book everyone needs to read. Our education and society would be so much better if this book was part of the school syllabus. It's very subversive and incredibly intelligent. Criticizes everything wrong with today's society and offers solutions. Unbelievable story, unbelievable writing. If I had to choose one book to read through eternity, this would be the one!

JOSH on AMAZON.CO.UK

Full of anecdotes about the film, its star-studded cast, the writer and director, and their struggles with the suited executives. Every page has a jewel to throw light upon the people behind the movies we love. Want to know what goes on behind the scenes in Hollywood? Here we see exactly what creatives go through to see their ideas brought to life by the mega-corporations. If you've ever seen Mars Attacks you will absolutely love this book.

WILLIAM HARWARD.

I found it fascinating that he and Tim Burton were able to take so many risks in this modern era of conglomerate films. His comments are a refreshing insight into a Hollywood which is in desperate need of being spruced up.

JUDE ZIETARA.

In Europe and South America, movies are called 'The Seventh Art.' In the USA, they are called 'The Industry.' After reading this insightful, funny, and sometimes shocking, book, I can see why.

MILANKO LUKOVIC.

A fascinating read about scriptwriting and filmmaking. I never knew how interesting the whole process was, and I enjoyed getting to know the stars and the crew. I was laughing all the way through.

COLIN PANRUCKER.

Mila Pop's lively and natural passion for people and their lives is infectious and fun. It will always leave you wanting more. The wacky Mars Attacks! is like nothing else, and so the wacky and hectic story of how it got made is fitting. The very touch-and-go nature of the movie industry is revealed. It can turn on a dime from gushing praise and promise to frozen over and aloof. Aspiring writers, directors, and actors take note! In Jonathan Gems, we see a man sustained by gratitude and the company of good people, self-possessed and of great calibre. Fully aware of others and soaking up the details of life. A true writer. He shows us that under all of the urgent and overblown dramatics and bravado of big movie-making are real people – flawed and brilliant. Generous with his many stories, you will likewise be left wanting more.

RO HACKETT

So very interesting getting new insights into the world of film and show business. What a clever man Jonathan Gems is too. So well read. I want to see the film again to pick up on all the extra things we now know.

DENNIS PIERCE.

This guy is amazing. He tries to tell you how we have no say or power when it comes to movies because of controlling rich people. Jonathan Gems you're my hero. Jonathan was trying to get out to the people that art is being held hostage.

TYLER on AMAZON.COM

WHO KILLED BRITISH CINEMA?
By Vinod Mahindru and Jonathan Gems

Reviews

Who killed British cinema? It's a good question – especially since us Brits used to have the second biggest film industry in the world and now it is practically non-existent. And the question gets explored with real vigour in this interesting and well put-together book.

It brings forth a mix of opinions whilst examining theories that could very well explain the 'death' of British cinema.

Not only is it refreshingly honest, but it is also very detailed, as it is richly supported by intriguing stats and thought-provoking quotes from credible individuals from the film industry (taken from pre-arranged interviews). Because of this, there is real insight within the copy and, as it has been thoroughly researched, you can find out more about the history of British cinema and its unfortunate decline in a succinct way. You don't have to pore over lengthy textbooks or wordy theories to grasp the timeline of events.

Overall, this makes for a riveting read that unpicks the political and cultural factors influencing media production and development over the decades and, if you are a film buff, you will particularly enjoy this in-depth piece of non-fiction. It even comes with a list of must-see British films!

HANNAH MONTGOMERY
www.whatson.guide

★★★★★ 5.0 out of 5 stars. **A Film Maker's Must Read!**

There is no shortage of resources for new and emerging filmmakers. There are courses, free and paid apps, some excellent and some not-so-good; there are many, many books written about every aspect of the art, from writing the script to where to stay in

Cannes when you're sending your new baby out into a world of adoring soon-to-be fans. All of these, to a greater or lesser degree, have their uses but if, like me, you are involved in the production of shorts and /or features in the UK, there is one resource that will make you angry. Very angry. A book (and documentary film) that will make your blood boil and – if you're anything like me – wonder why you decided to become involved in the obviously pointless world of UK film making in the first place.

If it doesn't make you angry; if it doesn't make you want to scream in rage; if it doesn't make you say: "This has ALL got to change!" then you'd better go and do something else because, believe you me, you might think you love film and cinema, but you most certainly don't!

The book *Who Killed British Cinema?* by Vinod Mahindru and Jonathan Gems, is an in-depth and comprehensive look at the British film industry – or rather, the lack of it – from its glory days when it was the second largest in the world to the present day where there is not one single British movie studio, and 98% of the films in our cinemas are made by foreign entities.

Now don't get me wrong, I'm certainly not a xenophobic Brexiteer Little Englander who thinks everything 'foreign' is bad; far from it. I'm a Remainer who has spent many years of his creative life in Europe, who loves the cinema of Bergman, Fassbinder (Rainer Werner rather than Michael) and Truffaut, but who also grew up with – and has deeply rooted in his soul – the magnificent films of Michael Powell, Emeric Pressburger, Alberto Cavalcanti, Charles Crichton and David Lean – not to mention Terence Davies, Derek Jarman and Peter Greenaway. Films that truly express our national identity; what it means to be British with all its peculiar sensibilities. Films that show our individualities and uniqueness in a way that the current diet of pap served up at the multiplexes could never hope to achieve.

The book examines the way in which film funding has gone in this country. The role of such bodies as the BFI, BAFTA, the erstwhile

Regional Screen Agencies, Creative England and, most interestingly, the policy of successive governments that have led to the demise of our most successful creative industry.

Read it. Watch the documentary. Listen to what the ex-CEO's of these august bodies say about spending 65% of their agency's budget not on film production but on admin and salaries. Read about funding bodies that fund production companies owned by members of the funding bodies who granted the funds in the first place. Do this and don't get mad, I dare you!

This is not a negative book, nor a negative film. It is rather a call to arms for every filmmaker in the UK to say: "This is not right. This has to change."

I found it inspirational. I found that, though my blood boiled at the sheer injustice of it all, it has increased my determination to succeed ten-fold. As Buckminster Fuller is quoted at the end of the documentary film: "You never change things by fighting the existing reality. To change something, build a new model that makes the existing model obsolete."

If you buy one book about filmmaking, let it be this one. It will change your life and, who knows? maybe just help you to reinvent our beloved industry.

IAN MCLAUGHLIN MBKS

Q

website: www.quotabooks.com
email: info@quotabooks.com
Twitter: @Quotabooks

www.ingramcontent.com/pod-product-compliance
Lightning Source LLC
Chambersburg PA
CBHW072044110526

44590CB00018B/3030